INDIA JUNCTION

INDIA JUNCTION

A Window to the Nation

Edited by

Seema Sharma

RAINLIGHT
RUPA

Published in Rainlight
by Rupa Publications India Pvt. Ltd 2014
7/16, Ansari Road, Daryaganj
New Delhi 110002

Sales centres:
Allahabad Bengaluru Chennai
Hyderabad Jaipur Kathmandu
Kolkata Mumbai

Copyright © Ministry of Railways, Government of India 2014

Copy proprietor of the book: Ministry of Railways, Government of India

Copyright of individual articles vests with the respective authors or the Ministry of Railways, Government of India

Copyright of photographs vests with the Ministry of Railways, Government of India or the respective photographer

Views expressed in this book are those of the authors and do not necessarily reflect the views of the Ministry of Railways, Government of India, or the publishers. While every effort has been made to trace copyright holders and obtain permission, any omissions brought to our attention will be remedied in future editions.

All rights reserved.
No part of this publication may be reproduced, transmitted, or stored in a retrieval system, in any form or by any means, electronic, mechanical, photocopying, recording or otherwise, without the prior permission of the publisher.

ISBN: 978-81-291-3268-0

First impression 2014

10 9 8 7 6 5 4 3 2 1

The moral right of the authors has been asserted.

Printed at Thomson Press India, Faridabad

This book is sold subject to the condition that it shall not, by way of trade or otherwise, be lent, resold, hired out, or otherwise circulated, without the publisher's prior consent, in any form of binding or cover other than that in which it is published.

CONTENTS

Foreword   7
Introduction   9

PART 1: ESSAYS

The Great Indian Railways   17
Sir Mark Tully

Imagining the Nation: Connecting India, Connecting People   45
Ian J. Kerr

Railways and the Idea of India   53
Sandipan Deb

Indian Railways: A Symbol of Nationhood   71
Sharmila Kantha

Railways' Filmy Chakkar   91
Jerry Pinto

Railways: A 160-Year Heritage   103
Gillian Wright

The Spirit of the Railways   129
Biswadeep Ghosh

The Magic of Hill Railways   147
Gillian Wright

The Lifeline of the Nation   173
Sharmila Kantha

Space–Time Convergence and the Urbanization of India   207
Seema Sharma

PART 2: RAIL TRAVELOGUES

When the Train Came to Deyra Dhoon   217
Ruskin Bond

The Winding Path to Bhutan 223
Omair Ahmad

On Board the Bombay Express 231
Shoba Narayan

Aboard the Vivek Express 237
Aasheesh Sharma

Changing Lanes 247
Kartik Iyengar

Kangra: The Land of the White Mountain 259
Premola Ghose

PART 3: PHOTOGRAPHIC FEATURES

Railnama 272
Chirodeep Chaudhuri

Delhi Junction 281
Devinder Singh

Railways' Filmy Chakkar 284

Blast from the Past: Advertising on Trains and Platforms 288

Contributors 293

FOREWORD

Railways in India have moved far ahead from the 34-kilometre-long stretch it began with in April 1853 in western India, to the Indian Railways' present day route length of 64,600 kilometres. Nearly encompassing the entire length and breadth of the country, Indian Railways is well and truly on the path of entering India's two remaining geographical frontiers—the perilous terrain of the Kashmir Valley, and the vast and remote areas in Northeast India. Spread over a vast network of interconnecting trunk and feeder lines, transporting 2.3 crore people daily and over a billion tonnes of goods annually, and employing 14 lakh people, Indian Railway is the primary mode of transport for men and material in the country. Over the last 160 years, it has grown into a mammoth organization, which is both vibrant and pulsating with life—the heart of India.

Indian Railways is a unique example across the world as a cheap mode of transport and also as a modern enterprise producing industrial goods of a high standard through its seven production units. Rail transport is environment-friendly and promotes national energy efficiency, reduces emissions and is an efficient, cost effective, less polluting mass transit system. The railways are the vital arteries of India and this is evident in its multidimensional roles. Be it movement of defence personnel and equipment to sensitive areas or participating in democratic process by transporting electoral staff in special trains or in Indian cinema, Indian Railways are all over the country. Be it as a character bringing in change into a village in Satyajit Ray's iconic *Pather Panchali*, or as a setting for *Coolie, Aradhana, Dil Se, Slumdog Millionaire* or even as a main character—*The Burning Train*, or *Chennai Express*—Indian Railways is omnipresent. The railways will continue to play an important defining role in the country's agenda for change.

It is inconceivable to imagine an India without her railways. Travel on Indian Railways is the best way to understand the country as the railway compartment in itself is a microcosm of the nation, her rich culture, her heritage.

The purpose of this book is to take the narrative of Indian Railways forward from a historical perspective to its present day status. Various aspects, some known and some less known, of Indian Railways have been presented by writers noted in their respective fields. The authors have taken great pains to unravel the railways in this exemplary collection of essays and articles. The lighter pieces, juxtaposed with serious, analytical articles, offer a clear insight into the myriad facets of Indian Railways. The Public Relations Directorate, Ministry of Railways, who has initiated the entire project and brought it together so beautifully and meaningfully, deserves felicitations. It is expected that this book will serve as an important resource and reference material.

Indian Railways has paved the way for the growth of the nation and is the lasting symbol of her unity. It is indeed a 'window to the nation'.

(Arunendra Kumar)
Chairman, Railway Board

INTRODUCTION

Indian Railways is deeply entrenched in public consciousness and needs no introduction. And India without her railways will be an unimaginable entity. Having entered the 161st year of its existence—undoubtedly a long time for an organization to survive and thrive—the railways in India have grown from strength to strength since the time of their inception in 1853, and through the subsequent transformation after Independence. History is witness to the fact that Indian Railways has helped the formation of the nation and thus cannot be separated from the country's social fabric. It has bequeathed to the nation a vast heritage—historical and architectural—and today forms the pivot of the national economy. The vast network of tracks has brought the country's various frontiers together, knitting the nation into a unified whole. The perfect example of unity in diversity, of history meeting modernity, of the rural-urban connection, of a common meeting ground for people of diverse backgrounds, Indian Railways is steadily marching forward towards the future.

When this book was in its planning stages, the debate which arose was whether to look back or to remain in the present or to look into the future. There was an insistent need for an in-depth analysis of the railways, the whys and wherefores of its status today, to perhaps contextualize its present with relation to its past and to find a way forward. The idea of a collection of writings emerged from there; different writers would surely put forth ideas that would give a different perspective on how the railways have been viewed so far.

This volume of essays, travelogues and photo features brings together an eclectic mix of writers, historians, journalists and photographers, who have brilliantly revealed each piece of the kaleidoscope that is the Indian Railways. From examining the history and heritage, to debating its role in the formation of the nation, to affirming its connect with people across cultures, to keeping pace with the fast moving images of Indian cinema and the railways, to reclaiming its spirit, to reflecting upon its socio-economic impact and its future, the writers have presented a balanced point of view.

Sir Mark Tully gives the great Indian Railways a historical perspective in the context of its inception, financing and progress. Ian J. Kerr rides the rails to discover the railways' connection with the people of India. Sandipan Deb summarizes its socio-economic impact on India. Jerry Pinto views the railways through a cinematic lens. Sharmila Kantha, while agreeing with the affirmation that Indian Railways formed the nation, debates the need for change. Biswadeep Ghosh explores the indomitable spirit of Indian Railways and its employees. Gillian Wright showcases the heritage of Indian Railways and the magic of its hill trains. Layer by layer, the writers have unravelled the various facets of the Indian Railways, revealing its core—which remains strong, sturdy and solid.

The travelogues—both varied and unique—capture the essence of trains and train travel. From Ruskin Bond's delightful retelling

INTRODUCTION

of the sight, sounds and experience of the first ever train arriving in Deyra Dhoon and Karthik Iyengar's ruminations on the leisurely pace of a small station and the friendships that can develop on a journey, to Premola Ghose's travels through the Kangra Valley on a train that meanders uphill connecting various stations along the route and Omair Ahmad's compelling account of travelling to the eastern frontier of India and then on to Bhutan—the diverse corners of the vast country are well covered.

For Shoba Narayan, it is food—the greatest Indian passion—that connects co-passengers as they travel from place to place. Her mouthwatering account of the Marwari aunty's delicious tiffin is tempting enough to make you want to partake of the same meal. Then there is Asheesh Sharma who invites you to be part of India's longest train journey.

This book must be read by everyone to get a real understanding of what makes the railways tick. The ideas and arguments will compel the reader to think about this organization which tirelessly and selflessly continues on its journey to make travel easier, quicker, safer and, above all, enjoyable.

'Railnama', the photo feature by Chirodeep Chaudhury captures the tragicomic drama of everyday life of ordinary people played out on the trains as well as railway platforms.

I would like to thank Shri Arunendra Kumar, Chairman, Railway Board, for his unstinted support to this project right from the start. I would also like to thank Shri Mohd. Jamshed, Chief Operations Manager, Northern Railway, and Shri Devinder Singh, Executive Director, Planning, Railway Board, for contributing some rare photos which have enhanced the visual impact of the book. I would also like to express my gratitude to Shri M.S. Mathur, Executive Director, PPP, for his ideas on the shape and content of some important parts.

Finally, the efforts of the entire Public Relations Directorate, in particular of Shri Siddarth Singh, Deputy Director, Shri Narendra Kumar, Shri Ashish Trivedi and Shri Sanjiv Gupta must be lauded for giving the book its final shape.

Special thanks to Dibakar Ghosh and the team at Rupa Publications India for ensuring that the idea of the book became a reality.

Dr Seema Sharma
Director/ Information & Publicity

A stretch on the Sahibabad-Ghaziabad section of Northern Railway.
Photograph by Devinder Singh, Executive Director, Planning, Railway Board

The Great Indian Railways
Sir Mark Tully

Imagining the Nation: Connecting India, Connecting People
Ian J. Kerr

Railways and the Idea of India
Sandipan Deb

Indian Railways: A Symbol of Nationhood
Sharmila Kantha

Railways' Filmy Chakkar
Jerry Pinto

Railways: A 160-Year Heritage
Gillian Wright

The Spirit of the Railways
Biswadeep Ghosh

The Magic of Hill Railways
Gillian Wright

The Lifeline of the Nation
Sharmila Kantha

Space–Time Convergence and the Urbanization of India
Seema Sharma

Part 1
ESSAYS

THE GREAT INDIAN RAILWAYS

Sir Mark Tully

Historians tend to be divided into two schools when they look back on the Raj. The schools have rather ugly names: 'meliorists' who believe that the Raj improved life for Indians, and the 'immiserationists' who believe it made life more miserable. One of the most common arguments of the meliorists is that the British gave India the railways and they brought plenty of improvements for Indians. The immiserationists claim that it was the British who benefitted from the railways and the Indians who paid for them. But India believes in the middle road and I believe the truth lies between these two schools.

The railways certainly bought benefits. Perhaps the most fundamental was the role they played in laying the foundation of independent India. It has been argued that without the railways the state created by the Raj could not have come into existence. Lack of communications would have prevented it. And it was that state which the Independence Movement converted into a nation. The renowned historian Eric Hobsbawn once wrote, 'nations do not make states and nationalism but the other way round'. If his argument is right, then without the railways there probably would not have been an Indian state to build an Indian nation on.

In a collection of essays he edited called *Railways in Modern India*, Ian J. Kerr, one of the pioneers of Indian railway history, has written, 'The railways were instrumental in the creation of a viable Indian state including its emergent national economy, a colony though it was: a new whole, a new political totality that could be imagined as such.' Kerr then went on to quote the more poetic words of Paul Theroux, 'The railways possessed India and made her hugeness graspable.' Theroux himself also said, 'The railway builders sewed together the entire [Indian] subcontinent with a stitching of track.' This reminds me that in writing about the railways of the Raj I have to include the systems operating in those days which now operate in Pakistan and Bangladesh. The Darjeeling Mail which took me on the first stage of my journey to school in that beautiful hill station passed through territory which is now in Bangladesh. The Frontier Mail used to run all the way to Peshawar, now in Pakistan.

> It has been argued that without the railways the state created by the Raj could not have come into existence.

But if we accept that Ian J. Kerr and Paul Theroux are right, and there will be many of Amartya Sen's 'Argumentative Indians' who won't accept that, we must still be aware that the railways were certainly not an unmixed blessing for Indians. We need to realize that the railways were not built to benefit Indians. The benefits Indians received were by-products of a system intended primarily, but not entirely, to serve the economic, political and military interests of the Raj.

The development of railways was delayed because the

Directors of the East India Company were not convinced they were in their economic interest and in the interest of British financiers. The possibility and profitability of building railways in India had been discussed since the early 1830s, but the first passenger train did not run until 1853 because the East India Company calculated the vast investment which would be involved, and was not optimistic about the chances of ever reaping financial rewards from that investment. In those early days, the English bureaucracy added to delays in decision making. Its malign influence was compounded by the length of time it took to communicate between London and Calcutta, the then capital of India.

Although British interests dominated the discussions that preceded the railways, it was acknowledged that they would fail unless Indians saw them as in their interest. The railway historian, K.R. Vaidyanathan, has listed some of the questions which were asked about Indians: 'Will they be able to pay for the fare of a ticket? Would they feel at all for the necessity to increase the pace of their life? Would the masses ever travel by train if it were introduced?' These were the doubts which assailed the authorities.

It took a dynamic Governor General, James Broun-Ramsay, 1st Marquis of Dalhousie and son of a former commander-in-chief in India, to bypass the bureaucrats, energize the lethargic East India Company directors, and confound the doubters. A short man with a short temper, possibly caused by poor health, Dalhousie governed India from 1848 to 1856. His policy of annexing any princely states where there was no proper male heir and his victory in the second Punjab war considerably expanded the area of India under the direct rule of the Company. So it was not surprising that Dalhousie saw the value of a system which would greatly help the government to hold the vast territories the British now ruled. At the same time, he was a firm believer in modernization and the railways were crucial if India was to be modernized. In the famous minute which he submitted to the Court of Directors of the East India Company in 1850, Dalhousie wrote, 'It is quite unnecessary for me to dwell upon the infinite benefits which the introduction of Railways into the several provinces of the Indian Empire is calculated to produce.'

The railways were crucial if India was to be modernized.

In his book, *Blood Iron and Gold*, the transport writer Christian Wolmar has described Dalhousie's minute as 'effectively a blueprint of how to build a railway network in an underdeveloped country designed to serve imperial interests above all.' Even then, it has to be said that Dalhousie in his minute made it clear that the modernization which would come with the railways would also benefit Indians. At the end of the minute he wrote, 'I am persuaded that in the firm, judicious and consistent enforcement of these few and simple principles, the government will afford to India the best security which can now be devised for the continued extension of these great measures of public improvement and for the consequent increase of the prosperity and wealth in the territories committed to its charge.'

Dalhousie's enthusiasm for railways bore fruit in April 1853 when the inaugural passenger train ran from Bombay to Thane, a distance of eighteen miles which it travelled in fifty-five minutes. It was a gala occasion and there was big demand for tickets. So the fledgling railway company with a name which indicated grandiose ambitions, The Great Indian Peninsula Railway (GIP), put on a very long train, with fourteen carriages. The significance of the occasion seems to have been lost on the Governor of Bombay, Lord Falkner, who took the Commander-in-Chief, the Bishop of Bombay, and other dignitaries to the hills just before the ceremony, and was criticized for doing so by the *Bombay Times*. But back in Britain, the significance was widely recognized. *The Illustrated*

Weekly of London wrote that England's power 'was never so nobly exemplified as…when the long line of carriages conveying nearly 500 passengers glided smoothly and easily away amidst the shouts of assembled thousands.' Also amidst the din of a twenty-one gun salute. *The Illustrated London News* estimated the crowd at Thane was a mile thick. Apparently the spectators spilled on to the tracks but there was no repetition of the disasters which struck the inaugural run of Britain's Liverpool and Manchester Railway in September 1830. The MP for Liverpool, William Huskisson, got out of the train at an unscheduled halt, ignoring a warning not to do so and was run over by a locomotive approaching on the adjacent line. By fitting all the VIPs into one train, the GIP avoided another disaster that occurred on the Liverpool and Manchester Railway inaugural run when one of the trains collided with the train in front which had derailed.

Calcutta's East Indian Railway, or EIR, was not so fortunate. The company might well have pipped its Bombay rival to the post if the ship carrying its first carriages from Britain had not sunk when it had almost completed its journey. But even then there might not have been a locomotive to pull the coaches because the ship carrying the first batch of British locomotives sailed to Australia instead of Calcutta—a clerical rather than a navigational error.

After those initial disasters, the construction of the EIR went ahead rapidly. This time the significance of the inaugural run was not lost on the dignitaries of the Raj. The most senior of them all, Lord Dalhousie, performed the ceremony. Unfortunately, the Governor General was not well enough to travel on the train. In the EIR's first year thirty miles were opened. That meant it overtook the GIP which only managed twenty-one miles.

The first stage of the EIR line from Howrah eastwards was longer than the GIP's initial line. It ran for 121 miles until it reached the town of Raniganj. The town was situated near the Burdwan coal mines. R.M. Stephenson, the British engineer who devised the first scheme for a railway in India, wrote of the 'handsome dividend' carrying coal from those mines to Calcutta would pay. He also pointed out the practical advantage of having the railway, saying, 'I am aware of the difficulties under which the colliery owners of Burdwan at present labour, from the want of these facilities, and that they are now, from this cause, unable to bring the coal down a direct distance of 75 miles in less than two seasons by the circuitous route of the Damooda [river].' Stephenson recorded that one company lost three maunds of coal 'from boats sunk and other causes incidental to the existing means of transport.'

Building the Railways

It wasn't only the GIP and the EIR which expanded rapidly. By 1867, just fourteen years after the inaugural GIP run, all but one of India's twenty largest cities were on the railway network. This expansion was achieved by the skill and dedication of the railway engineers and the endurance of the armies of Indian labourers they employed. Massive manpower was involved in building the railways of the Raj. One estimate suggests that at least eight million Indians were employed in that enterprise between 1853 and 1900. They worked very fast. When researching for a television film called *Karachi to the Khyber*, I came across the fact that the line which traverses the inhospitable Sibi Desert was laid at the speed of a mile a day—something which might make today's railway engineers wonder how much progress all their modern machinery has brought about.

Building railways manually in India inevitably presented problems for the engineers used to conditions in Britain who had to work with those armies of Indian labourers. The engineers found it was necessary to devise methods of construction which combined western with Indian techniques. So a new syncretic Indian approach to railway building emerged, an approach which married British and Indian traditions. Indian workers, for instance, did not like the wheelbarrows which Irish Navies had used as they dug cuttings, bored tunnels and built embankments to construct Britain's railways, so the Indian method of carrying earth in baskets on the head was adopted. It wasn't just tradition which made the workers favour this method. It involved employing more manpower.

Building the railways was dangerous. Boring one of the tunnels in the Bolan Pass leading to Quetta was so dangerous that labourers demanded five times their normal wage to work on it. On the Chappar Ridge tunnel workers were lowered from the top of the cliff on platforms and then had to gain their own foothold to start blasting. So many workers were employed on building this line that they ate nine-hundred camel loads of food every day. Sadly, all the risks the workers took, all the lives lost, came to naught when fifty-five years later one of the tunnels was washed away in a flood. Anyhow by then an alternative route over the Bolan Pass had been built.

Constructing a line across the Western Ghats between Bombay and Poona, now Pune, was only achieved by massive loss of life and mistreatment of workers. In his book, Christian Willmar quotes one estimate that 25,000 workers had lost their lives penetrating that formidable mountainous barrier of hard rock, and deep jungle which many engineers had declared to be impenetrable. Woolmar also quotes an official report to demonstrate the callous attitude of the railway companies and the government officials to the workers. In the report it is accepted as given that workers will die of cholera and fever because they are 'so badly provided with shelter and clothing'. The writer Arthur Burton has said, 'The notion that lives and the consequent loss of working time could be saved by proper shelter and decent conditions does not seem to have been considered.' The bad conditions led to a revolt by workers in the Western Ghats in which they attacked locomotives with sticks and stoned them.

The railway builders were not always welcome. In 1856, Santal tribesmen attacked engineers of the East India Railway. The cavalry were transported by the railways to mount a charge with unsheathed swords against the Santals armed with bows and arrows, and hooked knives. Pathan tribesmen did not approve of the Khyber Pass railway trespassing on their territory. The engineer in change of the project pacified them by pointing out that the trains would go so slowly they would be easy to loot.

Building bridges presented particular problems because Indian rivers have a habit of changing course and vary vastly in width and depth at different times of the year. In his book, *Bridges, Buildings and Black Beauties of Northern Railway*, Vinoo Mathur, former member of the Indian Railway Board, pays tribute to the engineers who built them, saying, 'The bridges built were for their time marvels of engineering in themselves and the substructures of these bridges have withstood the ravages of time and have successfully carried the growing volume of traffic for a century and more and have dealt, in recent years, with much heavier axle loads.'

The changes in rivers' courses led to disasters. Bridges were supported by piers or pillars sunk in wells. Vinoo Mathur quotes an engineer's report on a disaster which occurred while he was supervising the building of the bridge over the Ganga at Varanasi, 'During the afternoon of the 17th, when the diggers had been at work since 5 a.m., the water in the well suddenly rose to above the top of the brickwork pouring over the top. A loud report immediately followed and the brickwork of the stening burst open at the upstream end leaving a gap of 4 feet in width at water level... The primary cause of the disaster was a sudden and violent in-rush of sand.'

Problems were also created because of mistakes in the design of bridges. Among the mistakes was the design for the bridge over the Sutlej at Phillaur. It was found to be defective and prone to severe flood damage. The spans were too short, the piers too numerous, and the foundations too shallow causing, according to the Administrative Report for the Railways in India 1882-1883, 'much anxiety and heavy expense'. Then there is the well-known story of the unfortunate Captain Barog who committed suicide when he found that the tunnel he had been boring from both sides of a hill on the Kalka-Simla mountain railway did not meet in the middle. Fortunately for the engineers on the Darjeeling Himalayan Railway, the world's first mountain railway, finances were so limited that tunnels were ruled out as too expensive. The railway climbed by way of imaginative movements, loops and zigzags.

There is the heroic story of the courage, endurance, innovation, and initiative of the engineers and labourers who built the vast system that spread over India. But there is another side to that story which Ian J. Kerr describes in an essay in the Indian Ministry of Railways publication, *Our Indian Railway*, 'The darker side characterized by incompetence, serious mistakes, ignorance of Indians and Indian conditions and prejudice at the less thoughtful spectrum to intentional, and at times quite blatant speculation, peculation, mismanagement and malfeasance'. Corruption in the form of 'scamping', contractors cutting corners to increase their profits, was apparently a well-known

> Indian railways did expand over a diverse—and often very difficult terrain—at a speed that was not paralleled anywhere else.

problem leading to the failure of constructions. By the late 1860s, two thousand bridges, buildings and other masonry structures had collapsed completely or partially on the GIP alone. There were allegations that some of the work on the collapsed constructions had been 'very shoddy'. In spite of this darker side, Indian railways did expand over a diverse—and often very difficult terrain—at a speed that was not paralleled anywhere else.

The British engineers were heavily dependent on their Indian subordinates who did not always have a high opinion of the management. In his report back to headquarters in Calcutta, executive engineer T.N. Mukherjee complained, 'The map we received is not trustworthy. Rain and hail storms broke out some days and blown [sic] up all our tent(s), so the whole night we remaining under water, no shelter was procurable.' He went on to list other problems that he and his party had faced but ended on a triumphal note saying, 'In the villages smallpox and other diseases were raising but by favour of God we finished the survey safely.'

In their rush to build the railways the engineers didn't take much account of environmental considerations. Their embankments blocked natural drainage systems causing floods which destroyed crops and cropping patterns. Mosquitoes bred in the stagnant water. Forests were butchered to provide wood for sleepers and fuel for the kilns which made the enormous number of bricks the railways needed.

Dalhousie thought he had resolved a crucial question once and for all—what should be the gauge of the track which was going to weave India together, make it more secure, and enrich Britain? In his minute, he first reminded the Court of Directors of the East India Company that Britain 'fell into the mischievous error of permitting the introduction of two gauges into the United Kingdom.' Dalhousie was well aware of the consequences of that mischievous error because he had chaired a parliamentary committee set up to try to sort out the muddle created by the construction of railways in Britain with two widely differing gauges. In his minute on the future of Indian railways Dalhousie said, 'The government should now at the very outset of railway works, not only determine that an uniform gauge shall be established in India but that such uniform gauge shall be the one which science and experience may unite in selecting as the best.' There was support for the British broad gauge, seven-feet-six-inches, with some warning that trains on any narrower gauge would be blown off the track by India's high winds. But in the end the gauge was set at five-feet-six-inches. Dalhousie had wanted six feet.

Dalhousie's warning against multiple grades was ignored later when the Governor General, Lord Canning, accepted the proposal that metre-gauge railways should also be constructed. There was a sore need for branch lines to feed traffic into the main lines, but it was thought these lines would never generate enough revenue to earn a reasonable return on the capital invested if expensive broad gauge track was laid. So India's network of metre-gauge railways came into being.

The Question of Growth and Benefits

The geography of the railways laid down in India was influenced by the interests of the British. Their commercial interests led to the first lines being laid to connect the prominent ports of India—Bombay, Calcutta and Madras—to their hinterlands to export India's agricultural produce and import British manufactured goods. Opium was among the products the EIR carried to be exported from Calcutta. Raw cotton on its way to Bombay earned revenue for the GIP. On the way back the railway carried the cotton which had been manufactured into cloth in Britain. The eminent nationalist Gopal Krishna Gokhale said of the railways, 'the Indian people feel that this construction is undertaken principally in the interests of English commercial and moneyed classes, and that it assists in the further exploitation of our resources.'

British manufacturers of railway equipment were particular beneficiaries of India's railways. Between 1853 and 1947, India imported approximately 14,400 locomotives from Britain. Everyone else was kept out of the market. Countries other than Britain only managed to sell approximately 3,000 locomotives to India. Nor were Indians encouraged to set up as rivals to British companies. When Dorabji Tata first started to manufacture steel in India, he hoped the railways would stop importing British rails and buy his. Sir Frederick Upcott, the Commissioner for Railways, poured scorn on the idea, committing himself to 'eat every pound of steel Tatas produce'. The commissioner would have got terrible indigestion if he had tried to eat the 1,500 miles of Tata steel track exported to Mesopotamia during the First World War.

India's railways had to develop their own workshops for maintaining their equipment and as time went by the workshops did turn to manufacturing equipment. The first locomotive was manufactured in India in 1895. But at the time of Independence, locomotive manufacturing was still very underdeveloped. It has been calculated that during the entire history of the railways up to 1990, forty-seven years after Independence, only 2.75 per cent of the broad gauge locomotives which had operated were built in India, whereas 91 per cent were British. The figures for metre-gauge locomotives are not much more favourable to India.

It wasn't just the railway industry that failed to develop significantly. Karl Marx had confidently predicted that India would industrialize when the railways came, saying, 'I know that the English millocracy intend to endow India with railways with the exclusive view of extracting at diminished expense the cotton and other raw materials for their manufactures... But you cannot maintain a net of railways over an immense country without introducing all those industrial processes necessary to meet the current wants of railway locomotion, and out of which there must grow the application of machinery to those branches of industry not immediately connected with railways.'

It would be wrong to suggest that there was no growth in the application of machinery. The railways did provide industrial employment and impart skills in their workshops. Rudyard Kipling's father, Lockwood Kipling, described the workers in the workshop at Lahore as 'busily and silently employed in the care of huge machines which require constant vigilance and intelligent adjustment; sawing, planing and dovetailing with an accuracy formerly undreamed.' Not all the cotton was exported. There are at least three cities, Kanpur, Coimbatore and Ahmedabad, which claimed to be the Manchesters of India because of their cotton mills. Jute was manufactured on the banks of the Hooghly as well as in Dundee. But no one could claim that when the time came for the British to go, India had fulfilled Marx's prophesy.

As well as their workshops, the railways did of course provide other employment. In the early days, over 90 per cent of the railway employees were Indian. But the more skilled jobs which included drivers, guards and fitters were reserved for Europeans. The Europeans proved expensive and troublesome. In the collection of essays, *Railways in Modern India*, Ian D. Derbyshire, says imported drivers and guards were 'notorious for their licentious lifestyle, drunkenness and verbal abuse of Indians'. So eventually they were sent home. But even then there was an emphasis on recruiting Anglo-Indians as drivers and guards because their loyalty was not suspect.

In order to ensure that British interests were secured, the top management was dominated by Britons. The Acworth Committee set up in 1921 to report on the condition of the railways reported that there were 7,000 Europeans in the best positions. It said they were 'like a thin film of oil on the top of a glass of water, resting upon but hardly mixing with the 700,000 below. None of the highest positions are occupied by Indians, very few even of the higher.'

Geographical Strategies/Changed Geographies

British military concerns influenced the geography of Indian Railways. The First War of Independence in 1857, known by the British as the Indian Mutiny (Great Revolt), came at the start of the railway age. The army made some use of the limited EIR track but the trains' effectiveness was limited by attacks on them. Thereafter, the way the railways expanded in North India was influenced by the need to connect cantonments. In the 1870s, the dominant military concern became the unsettled Northwest Frontier. At the time of Independence, half the Northwest Frontier, the longest of the railways, was classified as strategic. Lord Roberts wanted the railways to transform the Indian army from a force limited to dealing with trouble in India to a fighting machine capable of taking on an international enemy.

Military concerns also influenced station building. Lahore station is the most prominent example of a station built as a fortress which could be defended. In more peaceful parts grandiose building were constructed to impress Indians with the might of the Raj, and be symbols of its invincibility. Bombay's Victoria station is the most famous example of this. Calcutta's Howrah, dominating one bank of the Hooghly, is another.

There was a third influence on the geography of the railways and it was an attempt to serve the interests of Indians. In the 1880s, lines were built to areas where famine was likely to occur to deliver grain to them. At the same time, the British authorities said they would use the railway system as a whole to boost the supply of grain by imports so that there was enough to send to the famine-stricken areas. But sadly the famine lines and whatever grain was imported didn't end famines. There were two serious famines at the end of the 19th century. During the Second World War, there was the disastrous Bengal famine in which 1.5 million people died of starvation and a total of 3.5 million died, if epidemics are taken into consideration.

Inevitably the meliorists and the immiserationists disagree over the impact of the railways on the grain market and food supply in India. The meliorists argue that the railways made the distribution more efficient and gained higher prices for the farmers by creating national markets. The railways did also transport perishable produce such as vegetables creating markets for them and enabling farmers to grow cash crops which were more profitable than grain. But the immiserationists maintain that this reduced the amount of grain grown and so increased the shortages. They also claim that the development of markets only helped the comparatively well-off farmers. They were the only ones who could afford the bullock-carts to transport the produce to the railheads.

> Without them, the three great cities of Calcutta, Bombay and Madras would have remained small colonial trading ports.

Financing the Railways

The original method of financing the railways cost India dearly. In order to encourage investors, the government guaranteed a return of 5 per cent on their investment. When the guarantee had to be paid it was the Government of India (GOI) which footed the bill. The railways, therefore, had no incentive to be cost conscious when constructing railways because they knew that they were guaranteed their return on capital expenditure. In 1872, W.N. Massey, a former Finance Member of India, said, 'So long as the English capitalist was guaranteed 5 per cent on the revenues of India it was immaterial to him whether the funds he lent were thrown into the Hooghly or converted into brick and mortar.'

The investors who profited from the guarantee system were British, the railway companies which were created were British, and the headquarters were not located where the railways operated, but in London. The directors who sat in those London boardrooms were all British. They often found themselves discussing minute details of the management of railways thousands of miles away, traversing a land so different to their own. In order to overcome the problem of distance and difference, old Indian hands were often appointed directors when they returned home. But this led to gerontocracy. In the collection of essays, *27 Down, New Departures in Indian Railway Studies*, John Hurd records that some directors were in their nineties and had to be carried into meetings.

The guarantee system led to so much dissatisfaction that in 1862, Lord Canning, the Governor General, announced very firmly, 'I will not guarantee a single rupee for a single day.' This did not prevent a 5 per cent guarantee being granted to the Oudh and Rohilkand Railway, but the terms were stricter than the original guarantees, and Lord Canning's pronouncement did lead to other methods of financing railways, including state financing. The state also entered the management of railways. Some were nationalized, some half-nationalized, owned by the state and worked by a private company, and some owned and worked by private companies. The tendency towards state ownership accelerated following the recommendations of the Acworth Committee, and by Independence, most of the railways were fully nationalized and run as one system.

Inevitably, the railways had social consequences. Without them, the three great cities of Calcutta, Bombay and Madras would have remained small colonial trading ports. Urbanization spread inland as well. At major railway junctions, towns sprung up where there had been no town before, towns like Itarsi where the Delhi-Madras and the Bombay-Calcutta lines crossed. Thousands of villages emerged from isolation, some becoming small towns. Villages which did not merit a fully-fledged station were given halts. Towns and villages the railway came close to but didn't quite reach, were given stations a little distance away called Roads, like Meja Road.

The trains enabled workers to find jobs in distant places, relatives to attend family celebrations, particularly marriages, and pilgrims to flock to holy places or festivals. Three hundred thousand tickets for return journeys from Calcutta to the holy city of Puri were sold in the first year the railway reached that pilgrim town. Although pilgrims provided substantial revenue for the railways, they were often even worse treated than other passengers who travelled third class. They, at least, had passenger carriages where conditions were grim enough, but pilgrims were often herded into freight wagons used for carrying livestock. A British doctor, describing a guard forcing pilgrims with their bundles into a compartment already grossly overcrowded, said the train 'swallowed them like a gorged boa constrictor'. In 1867, the *Calcutta Review* strongly criticized the overcrowding in third-class carriages and said, 'We saw it suggested somewhere the other day that the capacity of passengers on the Punjab railway had been calculated according to the weight of the passengers rather than their accommodation.'

It wasn't until 1905 that the government ordered the railways to provide lavatories on long-distance trains. The lack of lavatories caused one passenger to write to the EIR complaining that he had been caught short when relieving himself on the platform, demanding that the guard who had ordered the train to leave before he had finished should be fined heavily, and threatening to go to the press if he wasn't fined. As if overcrowding and lack of facilities wasn't enough, third-class passengers had to tolerate arrogant and rude railway staff.

First class passengers, almost entirely European, were treated with great respect and travelled in luxury, sometimes greater than all but a few European railways offered. Oscar Browning in his *Impressions of Indian Travel* wrote of the excellent food and service in a first-class carriage. The service included a barber who appears 'no sooner than you have passed your hand over your stubbly beard'. Passengers on the Imperial Mail that met the P&O steamers at Bombay and travelled to Calcutta had the luxury of a predecessor of the Jacuzzi called a needle bath. A bather stood between two vertical steel pipes, punctured with lots of small holes out of which jets of warm water were ejected.

It was expected that the railways would bring about great changes in Indian society. The greater mobility, the growing cities where Indians of different castes were forced to rub shoulders, and, of course, the railway carriages where they were packed together like the proverbial sardines, it was thought, would loosen the bonds of caste. But at the same time, the railways gave the British greater opportunities to practice the art of categorizing they delighted in. Their rigid categories tended to make people more conscious of their caste and make the system more not less restrictive. Certainly when Independence came, caste was still deeply entrenched in Indian society.

The railways contributed to racism by separating Europeans

from Indians. Europeans occupying first-class carriages made it clear that Indians were not welcome. Christopher Wolmar tells the story of a distinguished Indian lawyer who woke up from a nap to find his slippers had been thrown out of the window by a fellow passenger, a white plantation owner. The plantation owner then fell asleep. When he awoke, his jacket was missing. The lawyer told him, 'Your jacket has gone to fetch my slippers.'

So, what did prominent Indians think of the railways? In the early days they were firmly supported by the leading businessmen, including Dwarkanath Tagore, the grandfather of Rabindranath Tagore. But it wasn't long before critical voices were raised. In 1876, Dadobhai Naoraji, the first Asian member of British Parliament, complained that India was not benefitting from the railways. 'Let us have railways and all other kinds of beneficial public works,' he said, 'but let us have their natural benefits or talk not to a starving man of a fine dinner.' As the Independence Movement developed, the criticism became sharper. In his seminal work, *Hind Swaraj*, published in 1909, Mahatma Gandhi blamed the railways for the hold the British had over India. He blamed the railways for famines too, and denied the claim that they had created Indian nationalism maintaining that India had been a nation before the British came. The Mahatma also opposed the railways on ideological grounds seeing them as an integral part of 'industrial civilization' which he regarded as 'satanic'. But he still used the railways to get around India himself and spread his message.

In spite of the Mahatma's view of industrial civilization, since post-Independence Indians have taken to it in a big way. There is no doubt that they like trains because they keep on demanding more of them. The post-Raj railways have played a major role in the industrialization of Independent India and in strengthening the unity of the nation. So, it might seem that the meliorists are right. In the long run, the railways have proved good for India. On the other hand, the immiserationists could argue that the Raj railways enabled the British to retain their hold over India and retard its industrial development so long that the damaging consequences of this are still being felt. I, as I said at the start, come down in between the two positions, regarding the Raj railways as beneficial for India, but accepting they would have been a lot more so if they had been built by Indians for Indians.

The first narrow gauge railway in India, from Dabhoi to Miyagam (in Gujarat), with wagons hauled by bullocks (1860).

India's first passenger train from Bori Bunder to Thane, which ran on 16 April 1853. (This is the first known photograph of the journey.)

The Old Colaba railway terminus building, operated by Bombay, Baroda, and Central India Railway (BB&CI), was inaugurated on 7 April 1896.

The royal guests at the grand Delhi Durbar (1911) being welcomed at a temporary station in Delhi's Hamilton Road.

Senior engineers at a bridge site at Allahabad, 1929.

Nizam VII of Hyderabad and Lord Linlithgow shaking hands during his visit to the Deccan in 1938.

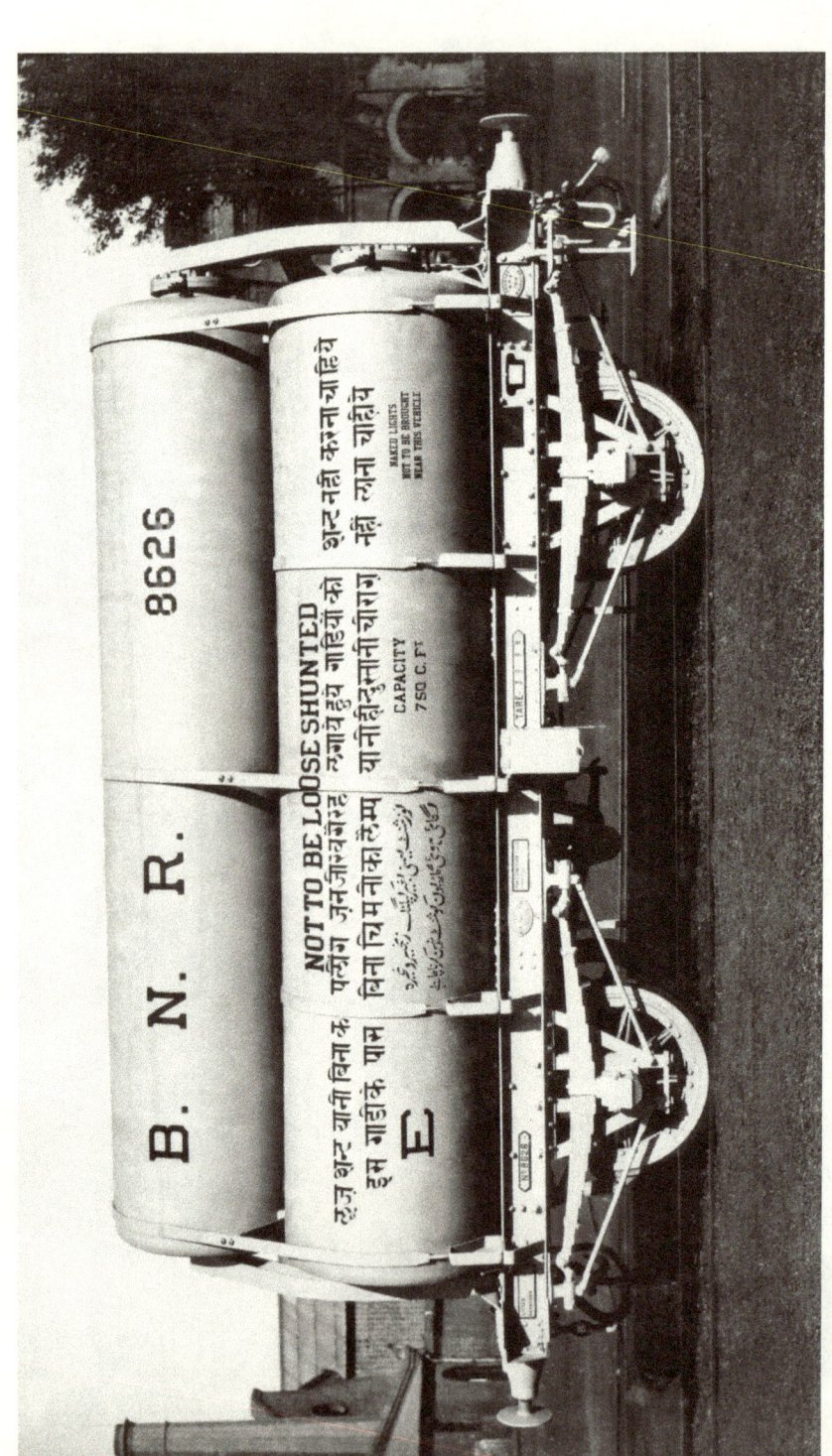

A triple-barrel tank wagon for petroleum products at Kharagpur, 1916.

Turntable used for reversing steam engines at Bitragunta.

National flag hosting ceremony on 15 August 1947 at Jhansi railway station.
Photograph courtesy: Mohd. Jamshed, COM/Northern Railway

IMAGINING THE NATION: CONNECTING INDIA, CONNECTING PEOPLE

Ian J. Kerr

In the mid-1880s the Indian political figure Diwan Madhav Rao (successively diwan of the princely states of Travancore, 1858-1872, Indore, 1873-1875, and Baroda, 1875-1882), exclaimed: 'What a glorious change the railway has made to old and long-neglected India.' He asserted that 'if India is to become a homogeneous nation, and is ever to achieve solidarity, it must be by means of railways as a means of transport...' More than a century later, what Madhav Rao believed was happening, has been accepted as a fait accompli. The railways, India's pre-eminent form of mass transportation, has contributed significantly to the creation and integration of the Indian nation. This is a claim, suitably qualified and nuanced, that finds support among more scholarly writers, and which is sympathetically endorsed here. Indeed, some historians have argued that without the development of a large network of railways, there would have been no India as we know it; in effect, *no railways, no India*. Perhaps so, or perhaps the assertion is misleading since the making of modern India would have unfolded very differently in the absence of railways, though it still would have unfolded.

No railways, no India.

Tracks to Nationhood

It is clear that the railways were enormously consequential in the formation of the modern Indian nation and its present configuration. The widespread network of dependable, all-weather transportation provided by the railways did integrate aspects of South Asian life within regions and across the breadth of the subcontinent. One example of this integration is found in the work of the economic historian John Hurd, who demonstrates the central role that the railways played in fostering the emergence of national markets in food grains, such as wheat, rice and jowar, and non-food crops such as cotton.

The railways in India were, and are, a large-scale technical system. The particular importance of a large-scale technical system—the source of its generalized importance well beyond the confines of what it is the large-scale system does (for example, the railways transport passengers and goods; electrical grids transmit a form of energy; telephone systems communicate the spoken and written word)—comes from the capacity of such a system to facilitate or sustain the functioning of many other systems. The railways of colonial India were infra-structural and structural. They became a giant enterprise but they also facilitated, sustained and linked much else, not only the commodity markets so single-mindedly studied by neoclassical economists, but many aspects of India's political economy and socio-cultural life.

Pilgrimage, one of the oldest and most practiced aspects of South Asian socio-cultural life, was deeply affected by the speedy, mass transportation the railways afforded. Railways, it can be said, add both mass and the masses to the practice of pilgrimage. More and more people—far more from the poor strata than the substantial numbers that already engaged in pilgrimage before the railway age—undertook pilgrimages, thanks to the railways.

Due to the ease and security of railway travel, many of these new pilgrims were women (regardless of the deplorable state of many pilgrim trains in the colonial era). Others were those for whom the quicker journey by train made pilgrimage possible in the interstices between demands for their labour. This became a widespread phenomenon that saw an increase in numbers, not only at the periodic Kumbha Melas when millions were in attendance, but also at places like Tirupati (Andhra Pradesh) or Tarakeswar (West Bengal) to which, day in and day out, year after year, more pilgrims came.

The railways came early to the Indian subcontinent—much earlier than to other parts of Asia, Latin America and Africa. By 1901, India had the world's fourth longest railway network (although the exact ranking can be disputed) as measured by route miles in operation, a ranking the country still holds. Track mileage continued to increase and reached an impressive 72,002 kms in 1947, the first year in which over one billion passengers were carried, with each passenger travelling, on average, 57 kms (total passenger kilometres exceeded 67 billion). In the same year, the last of the colonial era, net tonne kilometres of goods carried exceeded 41 billion. In 1993-94, some forty-five years into independence, total passenger kilometres totalled 296 billion and total tonne kilometres, 257 billion.

Colonial Birthright

The British realized early on the economic, military and administrative benefits the railways would bring in strengthening colonial rule in India. Indeed, for many mid-nineteenth century Britons, the railways were believed to be central to a progressive, British-imposed transformation of India.

Mahatma Gandhi, of course, disagreed with this assessment, arguing that the railways 'propagate evil'. He wrote in a memorable sentence that, 'Good travels at a snail's pace—it can, therefore, have little to do with the railways.' The much-travelled Bholanauth Chunder rode a train out of Howrah in October 1860, and soon after wrote that Hindus 'look upon the railways as a marvel and a miracle—a novel incarnation for the regeneration of *Bharatversh*'. Something of this transformation, or at least the discourse of progressive transformation and the belief in it, is captured in the postal cover and stamp issued in the early 1950s to commemorate the centenary of the railways in India. The postal cover represents a celebratory appropriation of the technological accomplishment of the colonial past to the project of Indian national modernity.

There was nothing altruistic about the British imposition of a colonial railway system on South Asia, the British discourse of 'progress' notwithstanding. The railways were an instrument, perhaps the central element, of colonial rule and imperial capitalism. Railways strengthened the colonial state. Gandhi saw this more clearly than most, hence his forthright condemnation, but in so doing, they facilitated the growth of an Indian state and hence an Indian nation, as they continue to do. An apt statement was made in this regard by the Polish statesman, Count Pilsudski, who said: 'Nations do not make states and nationalisms, but the other way around.'

Network for a Nation

Until very recent times, the railways were the primary vehicle of travel and social communication in India. The Indian Railways knit India together and made it possible for Indians, in increasing numbers as the years passed, to imagine themselves as a possible unity, a possible nation. (The railways played a smaller role in nation-state building processes in post-colonial Pakistan and Bangladesh than in the case of India, although they did assist the cause of Muslim nationalism before 1947 by facilitating travel and communication.)

Economic interchange and social communication, direct and indirect, was enormously increased by the railways. For example, the railway travels of the early opinion-makers reveal that they were among the first to imagine the national community. Diwan Madhav Rao's views were indirectly corroborated by the Bengali actress Binodini Das, who felt in the 1870s and 1880s that travel outside of Bengal was like travel to a foreign land. She wrote about the relief she and her colleagues felt upon their return home after three months of travelling and performing 'in the west' (which meant as far as Lahore), which she described as 'foreign lands'. Nevertheless, as with the Parsi theatre companies, rail transport helped to create a cross-regional stage for Bengali theatre companies. Much of India slowly became the stage upon which actors, actresses and audiences alike came to play shared parts, as did the 13,839 delegates who attended, largely by train one suspects, the annual meetings of the Indian National Congress between 1892 and 1909.

> 'Good travels at a snail's pace—it can, therefore have little to do with the railways.'
> —Mahatma Gandhi

Information flow is essential to the imagining of the nation. If train travel made face-to-face contact with hitherto distant Indians possible, it also made the critical, on-going, indirect contact provided by the written word possible on a voluminous scale. Newspapers, books, pamphlets and journals were distributed on an increasingly large scale, both regionally, in the vernacular languages of India (helping to strengthen regionalism), and crucially, for the nationalist elite, in English, the link language. The railways brought to the emerging national bourgeoisie much of their reading material just as it took them, or their letters, to other parts of India. The British took the distribution of the printed word seriously and continually worried about its potentially seditious effects.

Riding the Rails

However, the rosy, even triumphal, story of the appropriation of the colonial railway system to the project of national modernity, and the integration that accompanied railway development, should not be confused with the growth of an equality of opportunity for most Indians. The railways of the subcontinent, colonial and post-colonial, have been and remain instruments of capitalist development: combined yet uneven and unequal development, or what Elizabeth Whitcombe once labelled as 'expansion and induced imbalance'. Development and underdevelopment go hand-in-hand with capital accumulation in one area, matched by an over-accumulation of labour in another.

Transport systems connect the polar sites of capitalist development. Improved transport (including road transport later on) made it easier for capital to obtain and exploit those usually employed as casual labourers—the circulating labour of the intermediate regime between agriculture and capital-intensive industry so well-examined in the writing of the anthropologist Jan Bremen, but whose roots go deep into the colonial railway age. However, labour also rode the rails from the third quarter of the nineteenth century onwards to seek work in the emerging industrial sector of the economy. Men from the countryside of the western Deccan went to the textile mills of Bombay. Others from

IMAGINING THE NATION: CONNECTING INDIA, CONNECTING PEOPLE

Uttar Pradesh, Bihar and Orissa went to the jute mills of greater Calcutta. Improved transportation integrated labour markets but, of course, that did not mean that labour got a fair share of the value it helped to create. At the beginning of the twenty-first century, only seven per cent of India's labour force is in the so-called organized sector. The intermediate regime still predominates.

The full story of the consequences of the integrative effects of the South Asian railways on state strengthening, on the national movement(s) and on subsequent nation-building activities is yet to be written. Academic investigative research must be made which situates the railways within a sequence of communication innovations: the telegraph, the telephone, the radio, the bus and lorry, the airplane, television and cyber-links. Nonetheless, the railways were and remain at the infrastructural core of what made it possible for the Indian state and economy, in colonial times and after 1947, to function as an increasingly integrated entity.

The closing decades of the twentieth century saw India move increasingly from rail-dominated transport to road-dominated transport as measured by total passenger kilometres and total tonne kilometres effected, although much road transport takes place over shorter distances (and is, in terms of India's environmental future, less energy-efficient and more polluting). The railways continue to integrate ever wider areas and do so with greater efficiency. While India might not have become the kind of 'homogenous' nation that Madhav Rao envisioned more than a century ago, railroads remain part of the critical infrastructure on which the Indian state, nation and economy are built.

> Railroads remain part of the critical infrastructure on which the Indian state, nation and economy are built.

RAILWAYS AND THE IDEA OF INDIA

Sandipan Deb

On 16 April 1853, at 3:35 p.m., a train steamed off from Bombay's Bori Bunder station for Tanna, now Thane. The train had fourteen carriages and was pulled by three locomotives—Sultan, Sindh and Sahib. Four hundred VIPs were the passengers, and the train was seen off with a 21-gun salute.

It was a big event. The railways had arrived in India.

The public reaction was one of delight and amazement. Wrote the anonymous correspondent of the newspaper, *The Bombay Times and Journal of Commerce*, to be renamed *The Times of India* six years later, 'The whole line was densely crowded with spectators from the terminus to the flats of Byculla, tier after tier of the Native Town was filled as thickly as they could be by men, women and children... On crossing the flats and getting into the country between Mahim and Sion Causeway, spectators from the neighbouring villages were still found lining both sides of the rail, and thus it continued more or less all the way to Tanna.' The distance of 21 miles (34 kilometres) was covered in fifty-seven minutes, including a stop at Sion to draw water.

At Tanna, the passengers were treated to a splendid feast, the health of Her Majesty the Queen was proposed many times, and lengthy speeches were made. Said Mr Berkley, the chief engineer of The Great Indian Peninsula Railway: 'We have today publicly introduced...the most powerful system that modern invention has devised for the extension of commerce and for the promotion of civilization.'

In the next fifty years, the railway network expanded rapidly, and by 1900, the total length of the network (route kilometres) increased to 39,835 kilometres, which made it the fourth largest network in the world at the time. The rate of growth declined during the next fifty years, reaching 53,596 kilometres in 1950–51. In the next sixty years, since the beginning of the Plan era, the route length increased to 64,600 kilometres by 2011–12—an overall growth of about 20.53 per cent.

But the railways in India are more than just numbers. The train has always held a very special place in the hearts and minds of the nation. The scene where Apu and Durga walk for miles to get their first glimpse of the awesome steam-spewing leviathan in Satyajit Ray's *Pather Panchali* (1955) is surely one of the film's most memorable scenes.

Who does not recall the childhood excitement of boarding a train for a long holiday, the fight with siblings to sit by the window, the shyly inquisitive glances at the strangers sharing one's travelling space? The engine gives a whistle, there's the first shudder as the coaches yawn and stretch their arms—so to say, and then the train is in motion, slowly, and then gathering speed, well-wishers walking alongside the coach, still talking, mothers seeing their sons off giving pieces of last-minute advice, and then they fall back, and the train is out of the station, speeding away. As the child by the window looks at the houses and cottages and villages speeding away, he wonders who live there, what they do for a living? A few children come out of the houses and even wave at the train. The child waves back. The steady music of the wheels is soothing, reassuring and the occasional clanks as the train changes tracks gives one the confidence that the beast in whose belly you are residing knows where it's going, it knows where you want to go.

Of course, when the British introduced the railways to India, the principal reasons for doing so were hardly altruistic. Karl Marx, as sharp an observer of things happening around him as any in history, was quick to catch on. He wrote in the *New York Daily Tribune* on 8 August 1853—that is, less than four months after the historic Bombay–Thane journey (in fact, he had actually written his piece on 22 July; it was printed a fortnight later): 'The ruling classes of Great Britain have had, till now, but an accidental, transitory and exceptional interest in the progress of India. The aristocracy wanted to conquer it, the moneyocracy to plunder it, and the millocracy to undersell it. But now the tables are turned. The millocracy have discovered that the transformation of India into a reproductive country has become of vital importance to them, and that, to that end, it is necessary, above all, to gift her with means of irrigation and of internal communication. They intend now drawing a net of railroads over India. And they will do it. The results must be inappreciable.'

But Marx, with astonishing foresight, could visualize exactly what the impact of railways would be on an impoverished nation that was then little more than a vast number of clusters unconnected to one another. With the unifying force of the Mughal Empire long gone, India in the mid eighteenth century was thousands of parts without a whole. Wrote Marx: 'Nowhere, more than in India, do we meet with social destitution in the midst of natural plenty, for want of the means of exchange. It was proved before a Committee of the British House of Commons, which sat in 1848, that "when grain was selling from 6 to 8 shillings a quarter at Khandesh, it was sold at 64 to 70 shillings at Poona, where the people were dying in the streets of famine, without the possibility of gaining supplies from Khandesh, because the clay-roads were impracticable."

'The village isolation produced the absence of roads in India, and the absence of roads perpetuated the village isolation. On this plan a community existed with a given scale of low conveniences, almost without intercourse with other villages, without the desires and efforts indispensable to social advance... I know that the English millocracy intend to endow India with railways with the exclusive view of extracting at diminished expenses the cotton and other raw materials for their manufacturers.'

Cotton became one of the key drivers of the growth of the railways in India. At the time, the proliferation of cotton spinning and weaving industries in England meant that the regular supply of cotton was critical to their survival. In 1846, there was a major failure of cotton crop in America. Following this, traders in England turned their attention to India, one of Britain's colonies then, rich in cotton crop. Additionally, India's cotton was much cheaper than American cotton. As many economists and historians have noted, the initial advocates for developing railways were mercantile firms in London and Manchester, who expected the railways to lower transport costs and allow English merchants quicker and easier access to raw cotton from India. Simultaneously, the railways would open Indian markets to British manufactured products such as cotton textiles.

By 1869, almost every principal cotton field in India had been connected with shipping ports.

Railways also led the surge of development of towns, cities and, of course, markets of commodities like cotton and other farm produce. This resulted not only in the generation of employment within the railways, but also created new opportunities for enterprising Indian entrepreneurs and traders. The promise of a better life in these new centres also attracted hundreds and thousands of migrants. The profound impact of the railways on India's economy and agriculture even finds a mention in Jules Verne's book, *Around the World in Eighty Days*. The following passage describes Phileas Fogg and Passepartout passing through India's Western Ghats:

> Railways also led the surge of development of towns, cities and, of course, markets of commodities like cotton and other farm produce.

> Passepartout, on waking and looking out, could not realise that he was actually crossing India in a railway train. The locomotive, guided by an English engineer and fed with English coal, threw out its smoke upon cotton, coffee, nutmeg, clove, and pepper plantations, while the steam curled in spirals around groups of palm-trees, in the midst of which were seen picturesque bungalows, viharis (sort of abandoned monasteries), and marvellous temples enriched by the exhaustless ornamentation of Indian architecture.

A significant observation made in this passage is the reference to the type of crops being cultivated at the time. These crops—grown in large plantations (a new farming concept introduced by the British)—were meant to cater to the very large demand of these produces in England. This influenced more and more farmers to start growing commercial crops. The arrival of trains had changed the traditional farming landscape of India, forever.

Railway stations had emerged as nerve centres for commercial activity. Shops and markets came up around them and even the best and biggest advertising hoardings were often put up on the front façades of railway stations to ensure maximum visibility.

Then there were the new factories, which also needed to be close to railway stations in order to ensure not only steady and reliable supply of raw materials but also the transportation of finished goods. As more and more factories came up, towns started spreading along the railway lines, necessitating the need to construct feeder roads to connect village markets to railway stations. Almost every station had a feeder road, and, gradually, the railways took over the management of the roads.

> Railway stations had emerged as nerve centres for commercial activity.

It was not just the movement of commercial goods but also the rapid increase in passenger traffic that led to the rise in the importance of the railways. First came freight transport rather than passenger. The common means of freight transport at the time was the bullock cart, which could travel no more than 30 kilometres a day on India's dirt roads. These roads became near impassable during the monsoon, and for the rest of the year, traders faced the threat of en route piracy. India did not have an extensive inland waterway network. Coastal shipping had begun getting steam-driven in the 1840s, but this option was available, by definition, only to areas that had a coast. But trains were capable of travelling up to 600 kilometres per day and they offered this superior speed on predictable timetables, all months of the year, and without any serious threat of piracy or damage. Railroad freight rates were also considerably cheaper: 4:5, 2:4, and 1.5:3 times cheaper than road, river and coastal transport, respectively. This was a boon.

Of course, as for passenger traffic, the native populace initially treated the train with much suspicion. The thought of sharing a seat with a person of a different caste sat uncomfortably with most people. The prospect of taking a train journey with his wife or daughter—under the gaze of random males—would have kept men awake at nights. But Indians are, if not anything, smart and adaptive. The sheer convenience of trains steadily won over prejudices of every regressive sort. Also, the fundamental characteristic of the Indian civilization has always been cultural and intellectual inclusion. For several millennia, the people of Aryavarta and later Hindustan have accepted the Other's perspectives, beliefs, rituals and techniques and made them their own, till the Other was subsumed. It was only a matter of time before Indians realized the benefits of this new noisy giant technology and embraced it wholeheartedly.

Traffic developed slowly in the first decade of railway operations, but the subsequent increase surprised even official estimates. And as more and more Indians took the train, they were sowing the seeds of not only the struggle for Independence, but also today's modern diverse argumentative united nation and a vibrant raucous democracy.

Neither the railway promoters nor the East India Company envisioned much of a demand for passenger traffic at that time. They were, to say the least, taken by surprise. Not that they minded. At least for the first sixty years. But by then, they could hardly do anything about it. In fact, by then, the government had almost wholly taken charge of the railway system, and the government couldn't do much either.

> And as more and more Indians took the train, they were sowing the seeds of not only the struggle for Independence, but also today's modern diverse argumentative united nation and a vibrant raucous democracy.

In 1877, India was struck by one of the greatest food disasters in recorded history. The Great Famine of 1877, which is the way it is referred today generally by historians, spread from the Madras

Presidency up to the Central Provinces and even parts of the Northwest. It is estimated that five and a half million people died. Such was the outcry from progressive and liberal Britishers that a Famine Commission was set up. Following its recommendations, two new railway systems were introduced: the Southern Mahratta system in south India, and Bengal Nagpur Railways in central India, to alleviate famines. Greater emphasis on public objectives (in addition to military) is one reason why the rail network grew rapidly in the 1880s and 1890s.

Dave Donaldson, Associate Professor of Economics at the Massachusetts Institute of Technology, analyzed enormous amounts of data (the British government in India was very good at keeping records), ranging from railways and meteorology to agricultural incomes, from 1860 to 1930, and reached some interesting conclusions. He concluded that 'railroads reduced the cost of trading, reduced inter-regional price gaps, and increased trade volumes... (When) the railroad network was extended to the average district, real agricultural income in that district rose by approximately 16 per cent.'

John Hurd II, Professor Emeritus, Economics, Norwich University, and possibly the greatest living economic historian of the Indian railway system, was the first to make a social savings calculation for Indian Railways. He assumed that without railways, freight rates would have been between 80 and 90 per cent higher, based on the observed differences between rail freight rates and those for bullock carts during the mid-19th century. Using the volume of freight traffic in 1900, Hurd estimated the social savings to be ₹1.2 billion or 9 per cent of national income. This is a big number by any standards.

The railways connected people, connected cultures, connected different branches of knowledge. It was the greatest force of modernization and unity that India had ever seen. Yes, the printing presses had come, but it would be the trains that would carry the outpourings of an editor in Bengal to a kindred soul in Madras. India gained Independence within a century of the railways being introduced. If the railways had not been there, the British Raj would quite possibly have lasted much longer. Mahatma Gandhi could not have spread his message across the country so fast except through his incessant travels by third-class compartment of the Indian railway system. In fact, Gandhi could hardly have come to know the quandary, the diversity and the pride of his nation and his people so well, quickly and insightfully, without having taken the pan-India tour (under the advice of Gopal Krishna Gokhale) with his wife Kasturba—one of his first acts upon returning from South Africa.

> Railways was the greatest force of modernization and unity that India had ever seen.

Gandhi spent about ₹31 on his journey, including the train fare. Third-class travel, he thought, was the mirror to the plight of Indians. His meagre travel kit comprised a metal tiffin-box, a canvas bag, a long coat, dhoti, towel, shirt, blanket and a water jug. His travels in a compartment that had people from different castes and communities became a revelation. Indeed, one can say with some confidence that the 'Mahatma' was born on Indian trains.

After Independence, Indian Railways remained a critical driver of economic growth, but also consciously became an instrument for social good. Among all comparable transport systems in the world, Indian Railways is possibly the one most aware of its power to help the less advantaged and committed to its mission to create an equitable nation.

Where else in the world today will you find the Garib Rath (Poor Man's Chariot) Expresses, fully air-conditioned trains at half the normal fare for such travel on other trains, which is faster than the super-fast express trains? The maximum speed of Garib Rath trains is around 130 kmph, nearly same as the flagship Rajdhani Express' top speed.

Consider the Karmabhoomi Express, long-distance unreserved trains that offer a low-cost service to the millions of migrant workers, who work five hundred or even a thousand kilometres away from their village homes. A young man from one of the poorest district of India, if he has the resolve and the courage, can buy a ticket for the Karmabhoomi Express and travel to one of the country's richest metropolises and seek his fortune. He may be doing the same job, but his earnings could be four to five times higher. And he has the opportunity to move up the chain. Take into account the multiplier effects of the actions of this one man. This is how the country's Gross Domestic Product grows; this is how India has moved up from a low-income country to a medium-income country. All you need is a dream, a stout heart and a train ticket.

That young man could also take the Yuva Express. With a certain percentage of seats reserved for students, low-income groups and people belonging to the age group of eighteen to forty-five years, Yuva Express again offers air-conditioned travel at super-cheap prices. The fares with A/C chair car facilities in ten coaches range from ₹80 for the first 100 kilometres, ₹299 for up to 1,500 kilometres and a maximum of ₹399 up to 2,500 kilometres for youth who are unemployed and belong to low-income groups. That is, a young man can travel from Mumbai to Delhi and back and pay less than the price of a standard one-way ticket on the London Underground: £4.50 pounds, or about ₹475.

What role have the railways played in gender equality? This is a topic that has not been studied much. But look at the Mumbai local trains and no great empirical research is necessary. Look at the Matribhoomi special suburban services run in the major Indian cities—all-women trains—so that women can travel for work and pleasure within their cities safely and comfortably.

Ask anyone living in Kolkata, and you will know how women have been liberated by the introduction of the Kolkata Metro. Young women—not even working women, but senior schoolgirls or college students—can travel without stress to any destination. And destinations, as we all know, are not only geographical. Destinations are also in the mind.

Pilgrimage has bound the four corners of India since time immemorial. Indian Railways runs special inland tourism packages for pilgrims—a unique service in the world. And this, for all religions. For instance, one package involves setting off from the temple town of Madurai, visiting Mysore (the Chamundi temple, the Tipu Sultan mosque, St. Philomena's Cathedral), Goa (churches and temples), Mumbai (temples, churches and the Haji Ali mosque), Aurangabad (the Jama Masjid, the Grishneshwar temple, and Shirdi a 150-kilometre road trip away), Hyderabad (the Mecca Masjid, the Balaji temple, churches) and returning to Madurai. Hindu, Christian and Muslim pilgrims can all travel on this train to make their pilgrimages. This is an astonishing contribution to the secular spirit that is the sacred underpinning of India's vibrant democracy.

As of 2010, Indian Railways was building 114 sections of new tracks, 10,600 kilometres in total length, connecting the interiors and far-flung areas to main railway routes. The estimated costs were ₹69,500 crore. No financial returns were expected on these investments. Ten sections, totalling 1,490 kilometres, have been taken up as National Projects at a cost of ₹15,900 crore.

In the 1990s, the Konkan Railways Corporation carried out one of the greatest engineering feats in railway history that would bring enormous social and economic benefits to the Konkan coastal region stretching across three states—Maharashtra, Goa and

Karnataka. The 740-kilometre Konkan railway system, connecting the port cities of Mumbai and Mangalore, consists of over 2,000 bridges and 91 tunnels through mountainous terrain with many rivers, a region where flash floods and landslides are common. And the tracks allow speeds up to 160 kmph!

Currently, India is undertaking one of the most challenging railway projects ever in the world: building a line to connect Kashmir with the Himalayan foothills, where the Northern Railway tracks used to end. The Kashmir Railway Project (KRP), one of the National Projects of Indian Railways, is being developed to provide an alternative and reliable transportation system from the rest of India to the Kashmir Valley. The line is officially called the Jammu–Udhampur–Katra–Quazigund–Baramulla link. Right now, Kashmir is connected to the mainland only through road and air.

This 345-kilometre extension of the railway network will allow a 900-kilometre journey direct from Delhi to Srinagar. But this is no ordinary 345 kilometres. The route crosses major earthquake zones, and is subject to extreme cold and heat, as well as inhospitable terrain. The first section of the project, referred to as Leg 0, connects Jammu to Udhampur and includes 158 bridges and 10 kilometres of tunnels. And this is just in the foothills. This section was opened in April 2005.

The fourth section/Leg 3, which connects Qazigund to Baramulla, stretches 119 kilometres in the Kashmir Valley. It includes 704 major and minor bridges across rivers, canals and roads. This section was completed in October 2009.

The 148-km-long third section (Leg 2), which will connect Katra with Qazigund, is the most difficult challenge. A 1.3-km bridge being constructed across the Chenab river is the world's tallest railway bridge, rising 359 metres above the river-bed level.

On 26 June 2013, the first train from Banihal to Qazigund was flagged off. The 18-km-long Banihal–Qazigund rail link includes the country's longest transportation tunnel—over 11 kilometres long—through the Pir Panjal range. Till then, it would take people an hour by road—if there were no traffic jams—to travel from Banihal to the Kashmir Valley. Now, by train, it takes twelve minutes. As reported on the day of the inauguration on the website of the newspaper *The Hindu*, 'in cost terms, people will have to spend below ₹20 by train, almost one-seventh of the ₹150 that they pay to move through shared Tata Sumos.' And this will be all-weather connectivity.

Now only the 111-km link between Katra and Banihal remains to be completed.

The KRP will reap immense dividends for India. It will dramatically lower transport costs for regular commuters in the valley. A report in the newspaper *Mint*, dated 24 June 2013, quotes a local government employee: 'Gulab Hussain Bhat, a government employee, says the train service from Banihal will mean saving on commuting to Srinagar. "My children travel from here to Srinagar to study engineering," Bhat said. "They spend ₹100–150 a day, but now they will be able to travel very cheap. So ₹4,000–5,000 of our expenditure towards conveyance will be saved." The benefit extends to social aspects as well. "Our girls, who go to study in Srinagar, will come back home the same day," Bhat said. "Earlier there was a lot of problem. A lot of girls discontinued their studies because families would not allow for stay overnight or stay away from home. So this will do a lot of good."'

The new railway line will integrate the Kashmir economy far more strongly with the economy of the rest of the India. Even more importantly, it will bring the people of Kashmir closer to the other peoples of India. And when people come to know other people, they usually find that there is fundamentally not much difference between them. Prejudices are weakened, and relationships are formed. The railways in Kashmir will possibly be as important a

> The new railway line will integrate the Kashmir economy far more strongly with the economy of the rest of the India. Even more importantly, it will bring the people of Kashmir closer to the other peoples of India.

contributor to lasting peace in the valley as any other measure.

Another significant initiative is the Indian Railways' plan to improve connectivity between India's Northeast regions and the rest of the country. The strategically important 510-km-long Rangiya (Assam) to Murkongselek (Assam) metre gauge line is being converted into broad gauge. Other plans include adding the states of Arunanchal Pradesh and Meghalaya to the railways map.

It is hardly an exaggeration to say that, in a way, the railways built India, the way we know it. And as its continuing commitment to an equitable and integrated India shows, it is still at the forefront of the nation-building process. Its research on greater environment-friendliness—rail transport, in any case, is a cleaner mode of travel than by road—reflects its concern about the air our children will breathe, indeed, the planet they will inherit. The trains of India personify the spirit of India more than perhaps any other infrastructural facility.

This, when we have seen an extraordinary infrastructure revolution in our lifetimes—the telecommunications one. But what the railways wrought was as astounding, if not more, than what the Internet and cellular phones have done. They are only taking forward what the railways created. More than any other piece of technology, or service, the railways are responsible for India being a democracy. The railways opened up vast new horizons when we, the people, were dispirited, mired in poverty and ignorant of even our neighbours. The railway opened up vast new horizons, and paradoxically brought us all closer, gave us a national identity. An Assamese could taste idli, and a Maharashtrian could savour mihidana.

The transport system in India comprises distinct modes such as rail, road transport, coastal shipping, civil aviation, inland water transport and pipelines. Rail and road dominate, carrying about 87 per cent of the total freight traffic in the country as in 2007–08. Unfortunately, the rail-road mix in freight movement has developed rather sub-optimally over the years, as railways consistently lost out to roads, unable to install capacity or respond to market needs. The divide between the two modes became even more pronounced as roads expanded rapidly on the back of focused policy and investments, particularly during the last decade or so. The Total Transport System Study carried out by RITES for the Planning Commission in 2007–08, calculated that the railways' share in total inter-regional freight traffic had come down from 89 per cent in 1951 to 65 per cent in 1978–79, 53 per cent in 1986–87 and 30 per cent in 2007–08. RITES estimated that this consistent and unchecked fall in the share of railways through the years has cost the Indian economy about ₹385 billion (16 per cent of the total transport cost) in the year 2007–08.

That's another big number.

For passenger traffic as well, roads have emerged as the predominant mode for transport. The share of road in total passenger traffic (billion passenger kilometre or bpkm) carried by rail and road together has increased from 32 per cent in 1951 to about 90 per cent in 2011–12.

A number of studies carried out in the global context have

established that railways are more energy-efficient and eco-friendly than other modes of transport. Any shift of traffic from road to rail, especially in freight, would, therefore, result in substantial savings in energy consumption as well as reduced social costs. In view of the expected uncertainties related to the availability of future crude oil supplies, the implications for energy prices, and the adverse environmental impact on fossil fuels, it is essential that an attempt be made to maintain a transport modal mix in favour of railways. This requires making a strategic decision in terms of the relative allocation of resources by the Government of India between rail and road, and accompanying pricing and taxation policies that can then be used to nudge transport demand towards the desired modal shares.

These are the facts. As compared to road, rail consumes 75 per cent to 90 per cent less energy for freight traffic and 5 per cent to 21 per cent less energy for passenger traffic. Unit cost of rail transport was lower than road transport by about ₹2 per net tonne kilometre and ₹1.6 per passenger–kilometre. Rail transport emits 17 grammes of carbon dioxide per passenger–kilometre as compared to 84 grammes in case of road transport.

Accident costs on road are significantly higher than those on rail. In fact, for passenger transport, road accident costs are 45 times higher than rail; for freight, it is 8 times higher.

In terms of all-inclusive costs or social costs, railways have a huge advantage over road transport. For non-urban areas, the cost advantage of rail (in the base year 2000) was as much as ₹2.5 per net tonne kilometre and ₹1.7 per passenger–kilometre. All these figures are from studies initiated by either the Government of India or by multilateral agencies like the World Bank or the Asian Development Bank. They are credible numbers.

Today, one of the most urgent tasks we have before us as a nation is to invest in the railway system; strengthen, deepen and widen it, so it can, even better, serve the purpose that its original creators were possibly oblivious of. Trains brought us together, in culture, friendship and trade. They brought us together in nationhood. It is now imperative that we take it further. We owe it to the men who built—and still build—the railroads, drive the engines, solve the most difficult engineering problems. We owe it to India.

Not to speak of the sheer joy of grabbing the window seat before your brother could. Yes!

> Today, one of the most urgent tasks we have before us as a nation is to invest in the railway system; strengthen, deepen and widen it, so it can, even better, serve the purpose that its original creators were possibly oblivious of.

INDIAN RAILWAYS: A SYMBOL OF NATIONHOOD

Sharmila Kantha

The evolution of Indian Railways represents the awakening of a modern nation and is inextricably bound with the dreams of Indians. Today, it remains an abiding symbol of nationhood and national identity, a cherished institution whose presence across the country embodies our own sense of belonging as citizens of India.

It is inadequately recognized that an Indian played a role in setting up the first railway company in the country. We know Dwarkanath Tagore as the father of Nobel Laureate Rabindranath Tagore—what is less known is that Dwarkanath was one of the pioneering Indian industrialists at a time when modern industry was just beginning to stir in the country. Travelling on a train in England in 1842, Dwarkanath immediately sensed its potential for India. He set up Carr Tagore and Company on his return to Bengal and petitioned with the East India Company to be allowed to construct a railway line from his Raniganj collieries through a new company, Great Western Bengal Railway Company. Permission was not forthcoming as it was not considered prudent to have a 'native' construct such an important line. The Great Western Bengal Railway Company was merged after Dwarkanath's demise with the East India Railway Company to emerge as the iconic East Indian Railway (EIR), one of the great railway companies of history.

It is fitting that a great unifier of the country would use the railways as a vehicle for his national strategy. When Mohandas Karamchand Gandhi was asked to step out of a first-class railway compartment in South Africa, few could have imagined how this innovative thinker would leverage the might of the railways in India to oust an entire colonial government. 'I have now been in India for over two years and a half after my return from South Africa,' wrote the man who was to become the Mahatma. 'Over one quarter of that time I have passed on the Indian trains travelling third class by choice... I have covered the majority of railway systems during this period.' For Mahatma Gandhi, the railways were the best way to learn about this vast Indian land, a microcosm of all that it thought and represented, a symbol of its unity.

Few other countries in the world are as large and as diverse as India. Within our borders, we enjoy regional, linguistic, cultural, religious, ethnic and other multiplicities that together interweave the strong fabric of our nation. Such a country faces special challenges in developing its identity as a nation and several institutional systems contribute to crafting our perspective of ourselves as Indian citizens. One of the early and major contributors was the Indian Railways.

The development of the railways has been deeply intertwined with the destiny of the Indian subcontinent from the time when the British colonial government first drafted the note on its inception to today. The idea of geographical proximity with the colony through a new rail network was officially proposed in 1844 by John Chapman to the East India Company. Rowland Macdonald Stephenson in his seminal 1844 volume, *Report Upon the Practicability and Advantages of the Introduction of Railways into British India*, stressed the importance of railroad construction in eastern India to connect the Raniganj coalfields to Calcutta, now Kolkata.

Since these early thoughts, Indian Railways has expanded to carry one billion tonnes of goods and 8.2 billion passengers over one trillion passenger kilometres across the country. Throughout, this journey has been synonymous with the development and evolution of India, a notion that was perpetuated both by the colonial government that wanted to devise strong political unity as well as by freedom fighters who used the railways as a potent instrument to drum up support. A strong sensibility of the railways permeates our arts, across the media of films, songs and literature, a reflection of its position in popular imagination. Indeed, the unifying role of the railways is uppermost in this consciousness, which shows that it is universally seen as an icon of nationhood and national identity.

> The development of the railways has been deeply intertwined with the destiny of the Indian subcontinent

The long tracks that run through the length and breadth of the country function as zips, which interlock the country into a complete unit. This was not an easy task, but generations of railway men and women made it happen.

Background and Context

In 1805, the Indian subcontinent comprised Maratha territories, British-controlled areas, annexed lands and states under British protection. At the time that the introduction of railways in India was envisaged, the British had just subjugated the Punjab and would shortly go on to annex Oudh. The first task of the colonialists was to maintain law and order and smooth conditions for the conduct of business. The period of the first half of the 19th century also witnessed the first stirrings of nationalism, expressed as the demand for political and social reform in the Indian cultural context. Interestingly, Dwarkanath Tagore was one of the early supporters of nationalism, and formed the first political society, the Landholders Society, which included people of different religions, castes and languages, a forerunner of the role played by the railways. His dream of beginning the first railway line in eastern India could not be completed during his lifetime, but the line envisaged by him came up ten years after his death.

In economic terms too, the Indian production centres and markets were fragmented. Although trade had always been flourishing in the subcontinent for centuries and connectivity through roads and ports was robust, the level of interconnectivity was a far cry from what had been witnessed in other parts of the world due to the Industrial Revolution. The transfer of raw materials to production centres and thence to consumers was low, and villages were autarchic and self-sufficient entities, unconnected to the larger economy. A key challenge was the movement of food grains at the time of localized famines to the affected area, in order to prevent large-scale deaths.

The social context was equally constrained by geography, and the unit of interaction remained the village, complete with its various hierarchies, for most of society. The absence of transport and communication links left rural areas in their traditional modes of social behaviour, while in the urban areas, the hurdle was lack of literacy and access to printed material. Social reform was beginning to take place but the information gap made it a rather limited effort and the need for change was not widely recognized at the time the railways made their appearance.

Taking all these aspects together, it is evident that the transformation wrought by the railways cannot be overemphasized.

Indeed, the impact of this mode of mass transport was revolutionary in a way that few other developments had been.

To begin with, the British government conceived of railway lines in India as a means to strengthen its political presence and to develop a mode of transportation for its military contingents. However, right from the start, business leaders were key proponents of building the railway system. There were several reasons for this, including the fact that in England, railway construction was already quite advanced and the market for related engineering goods was seen to be slowing down. Second, British industry was looking for consumers for its surplus goods while also seeking the natural resources of the subcontinent. The idea of a supply chain from Lancashire and Manchester to Calcutta was highly appealing. Finally, the government did not envisage investing its own resources and was inclined towards looking for private sector participation.

The solution to attracting private sector investments was to guarantee a minimum rate of return, fixed at close to 5 per cent. Once the government did that, there was a high rate of participation from British companies in the initial years. In the first instance, Indian industry, too, supported the introduction of railways in the country, believing that this would take the country's economy into modernity as in England. However, later Indian economic analysts, including Dadabhai Naoroji and R.C. Dutt, pointed out that the huge sums being spent on the railways were at the expense of other important public works like irrigation. They not only decried the unnecessary losses suffered by the government in ensuring guaranteed returns, but also the fact that the amount was generated through revenues in India.

Notwithstanding this controversy, tracks now came up at a fast speed, especially after the First War of Independence in 1857 that convinced the British to scale up railways to ensure the rapid movement of troops. This followed the assumption of administrative control of the Indian territories by the Crown. By 1891, over 17,300 kilometres of tracks connected India, extending across the Gangetic plains to the Indus, and through to the Presidencies of Calcutta, Madras and Bombay, along interiors to resource-rich centres of cotton, opium and coal and right up to the busy ports.

While on the one hand this expansion created new avenues for political and economic integration as envisaged by the colonial government, on the other hand it also served as the vehicle for a new nationalist sentiment to surge on the back of massive mobilization and mobility. Interestingly, the railway infrastructure itself was to become a contested space in the national movement.

Political Impact

The Crown took charge of governing India soon after 1857, and the subsequent crackdown over the years owed much to the rapid movement of troops on the new railway system. The railway stations constructed near military towns and cantonments were designed in a manner that ensured smooth movement of troops. These stations were to be used as quick means of exit and as a refuge in case conflicts arose. The Lucknow station, for example, was supposed to act as a safe place for the entire European population of the city in case of a threat perception, and the country had as many as 301 railway police stations in 1919. The routes were also devised to connect the centres of British government in the principal cities.

At the same time, the fledgling political organizations that were coming up were able to overcome restrictions of distance and collect members from all over the country. David A. Campion in his essay on 'Railway Policing and Security in Colonial India, c.1860-1930', in *Our Indian Railway: Themes in India's Railway History* writes, 'It was only natural that the railways would become a chief battleground for the survival of the empire on one side and the realization of national independence on the other.' It is well-recognized by historians that the introduction of the railways helped to integrate separate geographical regions by compressing distance and travel time which in turn led to development of a national sense of identity and common purpose against colonialism.

Mahatma Gandhi realized the significance of the railways in the national consciousness almost as soon as he landed back on Indian soil. Hence, the decision to travel the length and breadth of the country certainly had much to do with his belief that railways by then had come to represent the spirit of India. That he chose to travel by third class was another of his remarkable ways to connect with the masses and won him immense support.

The mass movements that followed—civil disobedience and non-cooperation—depended much on railway travel, not just for senior leaders but also their supporters. Indeed, Campion writes that by monitoring the national leaders' rail travel, the railway police were able to tip off the Criminal Investigation Department about upcoming rallies and protests. The CID then presented themselves at the station to detain the arriving person and prevent the rally. Travelling without tickets was an accepted practice of non-cooperation and hundreds of thousands of people were arrested by railway police for this. Sabotage on the railways was also a form of protest as it was seen as a potent symbol of colonial rule. Thus, the

> The mass movements that followed for civil disobedience and non-cooperation depended much on railway travel, not just for senior leaders but also their supporters.

railways truly were a space for the development of the nationalistic identity.

Indian nationalists were hardly taken in by the British protestations that railways would usher in a new era of modernity in an ossified culture and economy. They closely studied the papers related to the construction of the rail network and universally condemned the objectives of the colonial government. The research works of analysts like Dadabhai Naoroji and GS Iyer on the drain of wealth due to the construction of the railways and other means were stinging indictments of the colonial policies and became grounds for rallying further support.

In 1950-51, India had about 53,600 kilometres of rail routes spanning the country. In the last sixty years, an additional 11,000 kilometres of rail tracks have been constructed. This is essentially because the government's focus shifted to creating infrastructure for other modes of travel such as roads, highways and aviation. As such, the railways have yielded some of their lustre as a symbol of national unity and identity. An interesting aspect of the modern transport system in India is that the railways' relevance as a mass mobilizer has diminished. The system of rail roko (stopping rail services), which was often used in earlier times by protestors, has become quite rare. In a way, this also reflects responsibility towards a public space where disruption could cause huge public dissatisfaction. Perhaps realizing the impact of such disruption, the Indian Railways have often been made a target for violent attacks by terrorists and insurgents. The seven horrific bomb blasts in Mumbai suburban trains in July 2006 that took the lives of 209 travellers and injured another 700 still ring clearly in our memories. Numerous occasions of tracks being blown up, signals being damaged, passengers being looted, and other incidents were cited in past years. However, since 2012, such violent incidents have come down considerably owing to heightened security measures such as patrolling by the Railway Protection Force, security checks at platforms, cameras at strategic locations and others.

Part of the shift in perception of the railways as a national unifier was inevitable because of technological change and advent of other modes of transport; still, for the vast millions of people who travel regularly on the Indian trains, the railways remain an indispensable part of their daily life. The role of railways has changed as India has matured as a nation, but its central responsibility in nation-building continues. Today, when we see a train chug past us, we all feel a tug of emotion and a thrill while we wonder which parts of our vast land it will traverse during its journey

Economic Unity

Caravans of load-bearing animals and heavy carts ambling leisurely along roads built through the centuries defined traditional trade routes through the Indian subcontinent. The emperors and kings of yore were characterized as 'good' or 'poor' administrators depending on the number of roads and sarais they built and the trees planted alongside for the benefit of the hapless traveller. The advent of the railways completely changed the economic nature of the country. Travel time came down from months and weeks to days and hours. The quantum of goods carried could be vastly expanded. Economic integration of a scale never imagined before was made possible.

There were several ways in which economic integration was enabled by the railways. One, it connected markets like never before, setting up supply chains between production and consumption end points, and making raw material, inputs and commodities widely available in all parts of the country. Two, it helped to develop domestic engineering and industry capabilities since construction and maintenance of lines and rolling stock required more skills and material than could be imported. Three, it offered huge employment opportunities to all sections of society, a role that it continues to play today as the largest civilian employer in the country.

Initially, all the equipment required for construction of the tracks as well as rolling stock, engineering goods and other raw material was completely imported from Britain. One of the reasons that the Great Indian Peninsula Railway got the distinction of being the first to run a train in 1853 was because the carriages imported for the inaugural train of East Indian Railway sank at Sandheads at the Hooghly river mouth, and the locomotive was mistakenly transported to Australia.

The pressure from British companies to kick-start railway construction in this vast new dominion must, therefore, have been quite intense. Investors, who received a guaranteed rate of return on their funds in the early days, were oblivious to the profligate use of machinery and equipment and continued to invest indiscriminately as long as the policy was in place. During the first fifty years of the railways, periods of rapid growth alternated with periods of slow growth, with the turn of the century witnessing lines being constructed faster than they were in England.

The first natural resource to be tapped for British markets was coal and Lord Dalhousie writes that the proposed line 'will run in the direction of the present very considerable goods traffic which is conveyed along the Great Trunk Road to Benares, and in the direction of such passenger traffic as is carried on by land and it will secure the carriage of the whole mineral traffic which now finds its way with risks and uncertainty by the river Damooda.' Jute, cotton and iron were other commodities carried on the railway lines. In the other direction, textiles, machinery, equipment, armaments and other commodities travelled to Indian markets, providing the unbroken link between the mills and factories of Lancashire and Manchester to trading hubs in India. As British goods invaded the country, Indian production centres fell increasingly silent.

A seminal contribution of the advent of the railways was that their construction ushered in modern production methods into India. British businesses started setting up production centres in India and lobbying strongly for railway procurement to source from local industry. Engineering associations, set up by British interests in the late 19th century, emerged as the rallying point for firms such as Burn and Company (founded 1781), Richardson and Cruddas, and Jessop and Co, which were increasingly involved in undertaking construction activities such as bridges, roads and public works. As in the textile industry, where British machine makers encouraged establishment of Indian-owned cotton mills—coincidentally, the first cotton mill was set up in 1853, the same year that the first railway track became operational—these engineering companies developed the indigenous industry.

As late as 1862, British policy mandated that all procurement, including for railways, military and public works, would be sourced from Britain with absolutely no local purchase. The 1876 policy allowed purchase of stores in the local market under the condition that they should only be of Indian origin, could cover only items that could be paid for on delivery and no advance was to be paid.

This was mainly to reduce the payment to Britain that in this year was 1.5 million pounds sterling. In the 1880 policy, for 'fostering the development of local industry', articles of Indian manufacture were to be substituted for European items 'whenever it is possible to do so even at some temporary increase of cost'.[1] The value of stores manufactured in India and substituted for stores hitherto imported in 1895-96 was ₹130 lakh. A Stores Committee was set up in 1906 and its recommendations were accepted in 1909. It allowed Indian mercantile houses to sell goods as well. While larger British-owned firms garnered most of the procurement orders available, a robust industry of ancillaries operated by Indian entrepreneurs came into being as well.

From these humble beginnings, railway production was completely indigenized after Independence, coming under the domain of government-led industries. Locomotive, wagon and wheel and axle factories were set up at various sites around the country, the idea being to become self-reliant in railway production. The railway electrification project and conversion from narrow and metre gauge to uni-gauge are major ongoing endeavours, entailing much effort.

Even though the railways came under the public sector, existing private sector firms continued production. Following policy developments, several of the private sector companies including Jessop and Co, Richardson and Cruddas, and others, became sick and had to be taken over by the public sector. A visit to Burn Standard and Company, a company formed with the merger Burn and Company Limited (Howrah) and Indian Standard Wagon Company Limited (Burnpur), some years ago revealed machinery over a century old still in operation and a few hundred workers

---

[1]'Government Purchase of Stores for India 1858–1914', article by Sunil K. Sen in journal *Bengal Past and Present* 1961 Jan-June edition

working a factory that spread over 140 acres in prime property in Howrah. It enjoyed facilities to produce all parts of a railway wagon except gearboxes but faced challenges in obtaining raw material and inputs. These large firms that had once been the pride of a new India are now struggling in limbo as sick units.

The railways have seen good progress between 2000-01 and 2011-12. Goods carried in terms of billion tonne kilometres that earned revenues doubled in this period, while the earnings trebled to over ₹67.8 thousand crores.[2] As this was the period when the Indian economy averaged a pace of growth faster than at any previous time since 1947, this good performance is not surprising.

However, the share of railways in the overall transportation profile of the country has been falling and is below 40 per cent. With the rapid development of roads and highways over the first decade of the 21st century, and lower airline costs, the railway system faces increasing competition. The Indian Railways are confronted with the challenge of raising this share along with building extensive new rail tracks, modernizing, financing, integrating administration among other measures.

Social Impact

Travelling in a train subsumes all other identities. Co-passengers in the same train compartment enjoy a bonhomie born of shared experiences that temporarily suspends linguistic, ethnic, caste, religious and regional identities. It is not unusual for train passengers to share their deepest emotions, life challenges, and concerns with co-travellers while journeying together for extended

> Travelling in a train subsumes all other identities.

---

[2]Economic Survey 2012-13 Table 1.25 'Operations of Indian Railways'

periods of time. This experience is well documented in Indian literature and popular cinema. Protagonists open up their hearts and souls to fellow travellers in short stories and novels, romance is still carried out in trains in Bollywood movies, and the enduring image of trains carrying the dead during Partition still resounds in popular imagination. When train travellers end their journeys together, it is inevitable that they part with greater understanding of, and friendship with, each other's social and cultural mores.

In a colonial India, divided starkly into political, social and economic groups, there was no greater leveller than the Indian railway system. As early as 1862, overcrowding in the third-class compartments led the wagon-builders to consider a novel scheme to double the number of passengers in a wagon—they introduced the two-tier seating arrangement, perhaps for the first time in the world.

In the early days, the railways offered a first and second class for government officials (presumably dependent on their rank) and the rich, an intermediate class used by less wealthy Indians and British, and a third class for the poor masses, which was famously used by Mahatma Gandhi to connect with India. An American journalist writing in the *Railway Gazette* of August 1911 described the first and second classes as being 'well-furnished', with 'soft and springy' leather seats, tubs for baths, and rotating fans to push cool, moist air through khus-khus mats. The third class, however, was not so well endowed, consisting of wooden benches in compartments divided by iron rails that looked 'for all the world like a travelling circus cage'. 'The poor unfortunates,' he commented, 'who are obliged to travel in these cages, are huddled together like wild beasts.' It is, therefore, no wonder that Gandhiji's travelling in these terrible conditions in the summer heat elevated him to iconic status among Indians yearning to be free of the colonial yoke. Some amusing incidents of his journeys are recounted here and there, although in later years, as he had to spend a lot of time on trains, Gandhiji upgraded to the second class, using his time to write prolifically. Still later—due to the huge crowds that gathered and ended up disrupting regular train schedules—the government insisted that Gandhiji travel in a special train.

As the freedom struggle gathered pace and strength, the flow of ideas and information was also transported in part through the railway system. Leaders of the freedom movement travelled through the length and breadth of the country, attending protests, rallies and meetings. Stations became places where people could see their leaders, and often were thronged when one of them passed by. Being the only mode of relatively fast mass travel, the railways naturally played a seminal role in the overall struggle for freedom.

Further down the historical trail, it is the images of Partition that we will forever associate with trains in the evolution of the Indian subcontinent. Trains packed with refugees, jammed into compartments, staring soullessly out of windows, and thronged up on the roofs steaming slowly across the black-and-white landscape of Northwest India, the horrific stories of murdered men, women and children, stations littered with bloody bodies—these are enduring stills that resonate in our national consciousness.

Today, the implications of rail travel go beyond mere co-existence in a common place at a common time. The Indian Railways has facilitated one of the largest inter-country migrations of populations. The Indian Constitution enshrines the Right to Freedom as a Fundamental Right, which includes the rights to reside and to work anywhere in the country. As many as 400 million people, constituting about a third of India's population, are estimated to have availed of this facility. According to UNICEF, such migration adds tremendously to 'economic prosperity, social cohesion and urban diversity'. Analysts believe that about ₹70,000–1,20,000 crore is remitted by this cohort, accounting for as much as 10 per cent of GDP of a source state like Bihar and adding considerably to economies of destination states like Delhi and Maharashtra.

It is the Indian Railways that offers the vehicle for such huge movements of population. The fact that an affordable and easy mode of travel between workers and employment opportunities is available smoothens out regional shortages and surpluses in labour. It offers millions of people a chance to go out of their villages to look for better incomes and living conditions elsewhere. Seasonal migration is a way for many workers to earn money that will tide them over for the whole year. This migration is accompanied by a massive social transformation, as the boundaries between rural and urban India weaken, and aspirations of all Indians converge. Today, the collapse of distance due to easy access through suburban trains and inter-city trains has enabled shift in mindsets, leading to social and cultural changes among the more connected regions. The extent of this migration has increased greatly over recent years, so that Indian Railways has had to put in place systems for handling the huge surge in travelling passengers during festivals and certain seasons. For example, after a stampede at New Delhi Railway Station at the time of the annual Bihar Chhath festival led to loss of many lives in 2011, the number of trains to Bihar was increased substantially to cater to the rush.

Domestic tourism is another avenue enabled by the railway system. Indians are inveterate travellers, putting together their necessities in neat bundles and suitcases, packing up meals for the journey, and travelling over long distances to see different parts of the country. They travel for pilgrimage, social occasions, festivals, or just for plain sightseeing. Over a billion Indians visited other places in 2012, according to the Ministry of Tourism, and the numbers are just going up. The large majority travel by train, and it is not unusual to see strangers in a compartment happily bonding over shared idlis and puris, sandesh and dhokla.

The Mahaparinirvan is a special train that connects Buddhist pilgrimage centres. These tourist trains offer a chance for Indian cities to benefit in terms of jobs and earnings, bringing new opportunities to young people in smaller towns.

The Indian Railways themselves are a unit for national identity as they employ a large number of people from diverse backgrounds. Providing living accommodation, hospitals, schools and myriad other facilities, the system like many other central government entities encourages intermingling of different social sections. Moreover, apart from direct employees, many other people too are dependent on Indian Railways for their livelihoods, including vendors, coolies, transporters, among others. By offering regular sources of income to millions of people, the railways contribute tremendously to social security in the country.

Conclusion

Over the past 160 years, the Indian Railways has come to represent the very ethos of the Indian nation, an entity that goes beyond merely a mode of travel to embody the spirit of a diverse nation of multiple dimensions. The railways have been transformational over India's history, and continue to play a central role in the political, economic and social life of the nation.

> The Indian Railways themselves are a unit for national identity as they employ a large number of people from diverse backgrounds.

Here is an extract from the American journalist's 1911 rendering of the railways in India that sums up its impact on national consciousness:

> *The railway has made possible a common standard of civilisation in India, and is knitting together three hundred million individuals into one compact mass of humanity with a potential energy for good or bad that no imagination has yet dreamed of calculating. What greater work can any human invention do in any clime?*[3]

Looking ahead, it is evident that the Indian Railways will continue to play a significant role in the future shape of the nation. Exciting new projects such as the Dedicated Freight Corridor (DFC) and high-speed rail network are on the drawing board. Accompanied by the two great trends that will define the Indian landscape in the coming years—urbanization and manufacturing regions—the railways would be the nucleus of a modernizing India. Already, twelve National Investment and Manufacturing Zones including many new, state-of-the-art townships are underway along the Delhi-Mumbai Industrial Corridor and other regions of the country, with the DFC being envisaged as their central lifeline. These townships would emerge as major manufacturing hubs, catering to world markets. The DFC would serve as the connector between the new urban agglomerations and global supply chains. Creating new jobs, opening new markets, and accessing new production centres, the Indian Railways have much distance to travel in the India of tomorrow.

> The Indian Railways are considered the lifeline of the nation, but more than that, they are the identity of India.

Indeed, the romantic spirit of the Indian Railways lives on, and each of us Indians thinks of the railways as our own special space that defines the way that we think about ourselves, our nationalism and

---

[3] http://www.irfca.org/docs/history/railway-gazette-railways-india-1911.html

our country. As our trains embark on their journeys, we cannot help but think of their destinations, near and far, that are part of this vast land to which we belong. The Indian Railways are considered the lifeline of the nation, but more than that, they are the identity of India.

Select References

Aguiar, Marian, *Tracking Modernity: India's Railway and the Culture of Mobility* University of Minnesota Press, 2011
Working Group Report for the XIIth Plan: Railway Sector
Annual Report and Accounts 2011-12
Desai, A.R., *Social Background of Indian Nationalism* 6th Edition, Popular Prakashan, 1948
Srinivasan, Roopa, Tiwari, Manish and Silas, Sandeep ed. *Our Indian Railways: Themes in India's Railway History*, Foundation Books, 2006
'Government Purchase of Stores for India 1858-1914', article by Sunil K. Sen in journal *Bengal Past and Present* 1961 Jan-June edition
UNESCO, 'Social Inclusion of Internal Migrants in India'

RAILWAYS' FILMY CHAKKAR

Jerry Pinto

When I was growing up in the 1970s, every train journey was epic. The tickets were to be booked months in advance and my father brought them home—small bamboo-coloured rough things the size of a razor blade—in his chor pocket, tucked against his tummy, safe from thieves. You started packing a week in advance. You could not wear that shirt today because you might need it on holiday and who could be sure if it could be washed and dried and ironed in time? The holdall had to be taken down from the top of the cupboard and its belts and buckles examined for the depredations of time and vermin. The suitcase was unearthed and unpacked. Yes, unpacked because an empty suitcase in a small flat is simply a waste of space. Once it was unpacked, it had to be packed again.

The railway stations were epic too, rich in drama, as we duly noted in our essays, 'A Visit to the Railway Station', 300 words, 10 marks, please write clearly, marks will be deducted for lack of punctuation and poor spelling. Wherever there is rich drama, could Bollywood be far behind? There were hoardings all over, big colourful reproachful actors staring down at us. 'You did not see my film?' Jeetendra seems to be asking. 'And how could you miss mine?' Sunil Dutt was echoing. If indeed that was Sunil Dutt, that huge purple face with the silky Chinese-looking hair. Meanwhile, my father would be buying bananas. (We carried our own water; there was no water to be bought on railway stations though up-country water was deemed safe as long as you had washed the tap with a soap-nut and let it run for a few seconds.) My sister or I would suggest a film magazine and permission would be granted. This was now precious and we would squabble amicably over who got to read it first. If I did I would start 'leaking' stories, generally lines that made almost no sense to me. 'Rekha says that Rajesh Khanna called her a…' and my sister would begin to hum and stick her fingers in her ears so as not to hear any of it. And when we were finished with our leisurely perusal, the 'auntie' on the next berth would ask for it with barely disguised avidity and plunge right in, reading everything from the gossip at the beginning to the letters at the end. Eventually many of the people in that compartment would have read the magazine. Even those who did not speak or read English would have a go, because looking at a magazine is also part of the fun. Perhaps they knew all the stars and all the innuendoes; I remember feeling that I was peeking into a world that had its own laws, its own nicknames, its own hierarchies and one that was so assured of its fascination for the rest of the world that it did not need to explain any of it.

But this was also the time when going to the movies was epic, an expedition. The whole family was involved because this was the time when you could not own movies, there were no video cassettes. You could only catch a movie—and the phrase was apposite because they seemed forever to be eluding us—when some theatre owner decided that it was worth his while. Train travel and film going: both epic, both exciting.

You don't have to be a film buff to remember that cinema has been fascinated by trains for a long time too. We all know that one of the first films ever was that of the arrival of the train and the sight—without sound—of a train arriving caused pandemonium among the first viewers who, we are told, scampered to escape being crushed. Indian cinema has not been exempt from this fascination either perhaps because, for the longest time, the train was the symbol of modernity, community and nationhood. When Apu and Durga run through a field of kaashphool in *Pather Panchali* (Satyajit Ray, 1955), flowers that are evanescent and temporary as our nostalgic memory of the childhood innocence we never had—and which we read onto the rural idyll, they are hurtling forward into the future, running to greet the city. The song of the little stone road will be obliterated by the roar of the iron road that runs through the flowers, bringing invitations to the celebration of modernity that is the city. The countryside cannot resist. Mahatma Gandhi was, therefore, not very sure about the gift of the railways. He said: 'If we do not rush about from place to place by means of railways and such other conveniences, much of the confusion that arises would be obviated. God set a limit to man's locomotive ambition in the construction of his body.' Although his own epiphany happened in a first-class railways compartment in South Africa, he used the third-class railway compartment during the Indian freedom struggle. The film *Gandhi* (Richard Attenborough, 1982) makes great use of this: Gandhi, on the top of the railway carriage as he begins to tour the country, on the advice of Gopal Krishna Gokhale, trying to understand India.

This was how the train was generally used in Hindi films. There was stock footage that could always be deployed to suggest a change of location. You only had to catch sight of a train passing and everyone knew that something drastic had happened. It symbolized a move away from a state of innocence. It said: 'Here is someone who is done with the village and must now seek his fortune in the city.' Whether he was played by Saigal (the 1936 version directed by Pramathesh Barua) or Dilip Kumar (the 1955 version directed by Bimal Roy) or Shah Rukh Khan (the 2002 version directed by Sanjay Leela Bhansali), Devdas departs for the city taking his broken heart and his seared masculinity with him in a train. Rajesh Khanna wanders into a series of trains with his broken heart in *Aap ki Kasam* (J. Om Prakash, 1974) telling us: *Zindagi ke safar mein guzar jaate hain jo muqam, woh phir nahin aate.* (In the journey of life, there's no turning back.)

But trains are also liminal spaces. They do not belong to you, except for the time specified on your ticket. This means that for the average Indian, concerned with notions of purity and pollution, they are areas of great suspicion, rather like hotels. This is where you will be accosted by the love of your life, only she's a dancing girl in a kotha and she's asleep. Only her foot, shaking gently because of the motion of the train… and he leaves her a note, *Aap ke paaon bahut haseen hain. Inhe zameen par mat utariyega; maile ho jaayenge.* (Your feet are beautiful. Do not let them touch the ground; they will get dirty!) Of course we know and she knows and he knows that she must put her foot on the ground at some point. What he does not know, not at this point at any rate, is that she is already besmirched, and that the only Pakeezah ('pure' woman) in the film was not Meena Kumari but the young girl who watches Sahibjan's doli leaving the kotha. Later, the plaintive sound of the whistle of a train will sound in the fading lines of one of the most romantic of *Pakeezah*'s songs (Kamal Amrohi, 1971): *Yunhi koi mil gaya tha sar-e-raah chalte chalte.* (An untranslatable line, it suggests a meeting that was not planned, no, an encounter that happened as she was going her way…yes, the ellipsis are part of the translation.) The rest of the film is so carefully decadent, so ripe with florid romanticism, with ellipsis, that this touch of realism seems to be almost a startling risk, a suggestion that there was a real world outside.

But love is that anarchic force that can survive the railways. It will disrupt the social order as surely as railway-booking systems did. You could not tell who would be sitting next to you and this forced Brahmin and Dalit and Christian and Muslim into close proximity, into a sharing of family stories and home remedies, even perhaps food and water, for dozens of hours. In Mumbai locals, there is even a new subgroup of intimacy: the train friend. When a friend of mine was missing from her train for several weeks—her husband had suffered a terrible road accident that left him bedridden—her train friends came to the office to enquire after her. Several of them turned up which meant they were probably missing work or at least going to risk reporting late. They went later to the hospital and they even collected some money for his treatment. The trains of my city may carry people in conditions that are not ideal but they still have room for a little humanity.

Not that this is ever reflected in Bollywood's depictions of trains. In *Zanjeer* (Prakash Mehra, 1973), the only witness to a crime is bumped off rather efficiently with the help of a burning cigarette. The drunk (played by Keshto Mukherjee) is at the door, dozing and dreaming when the villains burn the hand with which he is holding on to the train. He falls off and Amitabh Bachchan (again) must find another way to prove his innocence and regain his uniform. There he is again, our man on the trains, in *Shakti* (Ramesh Sippy, 1982), this time defending the honour of a young woman (Smita Patil) who is travelling alone. The fight in the train compartment is followed by a rare downtime stroll with the young woman who has been rescued.

In *Ek Chaalis Ki Last Local* (Sanjay Khaduri, 2007), the train is present as an absence. It is the train that the Abhay Deol character misses that causes all the problems. And so it was left to a Marathi film to actually recognize the impact that the trains have on our lives and our self-respect. *Dombivali Fast* (Nishikant Kamat, 2005) uses the concept of the 'fourth seat' to illustrate how close everyone in a city is to the edge. The railway compartments of local trains are constructed to seat three. But at peak times, everyone is expected to 'adjust' and move in a little and allow a fourth person space to sit. This can sometimes be denied, causing ugly altercations. Kamat's protagonist can no longer take his position on the fourth seat of a Dombivali fast train and he snaps and turns vigilante.

And so it is also on a train that one might go to die. The train is in constant motion, never stopping, and to a rooted nation where addresses never change over generations, this might be seen as a vision of hell. Where would you take your conscience if you were a union leader who had let down your union because harm is threatened to your wife and family? In *Deewaar* (Yash Chopra, 1975), that's where the missing father goes and that's where he dies.

But it is also on a train that a man may come back to life. *Jab We Met* (Imtiaz Ali, 2007) makes a break from all those movies in which a reunion is staged at an airport. For a long while, airports were the places that marked the break with ordinary levels of sophistication. In the 1970s, ordinary people took the train but airports were filled with smugglers who passed each other identical bags, heroes in improbable disguises, and Helen who could be passed off as Parveen Babi so that Pran could take his daughter home. Where else but in *Amar Akbar Anthony* (Manmohan Desai, 1977)? This is also the film in which you can see the toy-est of all toy trains, in which Neetu Singh and Rishi Kapoor sing their section of *Humko tumse ho gaya hai pyaar*. As Mumbai children we loved watching the toy train from the Sanjay Gandhi National Park whisk these two ever-adolescent lovers around its set destination. Amitabh and Parveen got a yacht while Vinod Khanna and Shabana Azmi got a clothesline. (No really.) You could argue that the return to a train in *Jab We Met* is a plot device. A man cannot take an airplane on a whim, not even a broken-hearted gazillionaire. A young woman in search of love would hark back to the trains, in memoriam of all the train sequences that have presaged love among the bogies. It could also be a retro-chic choice, a deliberate harking back to *Dilwaale Dulhaniya Le Jaayenge* (Aditya Chopra, 1995) played out on the railway systems of a continent and a subcontinent. Or it could simply be that the train produces an intimacy that the airplane cannot. You cannot move around on an airplane. You are seated in one place and the other protagonist in another. Your movements are hampered and restricted except in very special sections and on very special flights. In a train, you can move from seat to seat naturally and without let or hindrance. This means that while action is limited, you can still have a lot of fun. You can hang out of an Indian train and sing as Saif Ali Khan does in *Parineeta* (Pradeep Sarkar, 2005). You can drive alongside and sing a song to the queen of your dreams, your *sapnon ki rani*, as Rajesh Khanna does with Sharmila Tagore in *Aradhana* (Shakti Samanta, 1969). (La Tagore is reading an Alistair Maclean novel throughout. It's *Where Eight Bells Toll*. Why should you bother if the book has a helicopter on the cover? I don't.)

The train song should be a genre in itself. I remember the sense of surprise I felt when I first saw *Dhanno ki aankhon mein* (In Dhanno's eyes) from *Kitab* (Sampooran Singh Gulzar, 1977). Bollywood music is the white noise of Mumbai life. One hears the song, one even learns some of the lyrics without trying and then while one is watching a film, a rerun or a movie on the telly, there it is, familiar and unfamiliar at the same time. I had always imagined that this would be a disco kind of song, some intense young man singing it to his beloved. Instead it's set on a train and it wins one of my awards for oddest picturization.

Of course, most of the songs of *The Burning Train* (Ravi Chopra, 1979) are sung on board the train that is on fire. *Pal do pal ka saath hamaara* (We will be together for only a little while), Neetu Singh and Jeetendra sing and you're nodding because that is the intimacy of the train journey extended as a metaphor for life—and which journey cannot? The film had Dharmendra and Vinod Khanna and Parveen Babi and Hema Malini and Danny Denzongpa and a host of other small-time stars. The last song on board was led by Simi Garewal as a schoolteacher: *Teri hai zameen, tera aasmaan, tu bada meherbaan tu bakshish kar* (Yours is the land, yours is the sky, Of your generosity, answer our prayer), a beautiful hymn to the gods above. Those prayers did not work. The film crashed and burned at the box office. It had been touted as India's first disaster movie and although *Kaala Patthar* (Yash Chopra, 1979) had predated it by a year, that hadn't worked either. The coal that floated in the flooding mine had nothing to do with its failure; perhaps it was just the casting of Amitabh Bachchan as a Conradian figure, a Lord Jim whose battles were all internal, that did not work. Either way, a genre failed to take off.

The film, however, that uses trains to best effect is *Sholay* (Ramesh Sippy, 1975). There's a great sequence in the opening when the dacoits attack the train and the inspector (Sanjeev Kumar) must make a decision about letting Jai (Amitabh Bachchan) and Veeru (Dharmendra) free to help him ward off the attack. This was beautifully picturized and elegantly shot and written. Forever inscribed in my memory is the way in which Veeru is created. He had a long and hectic battle with some dacoit and finally manages to beat him off. And

> The film, however, that uses trains to best effect is *Sholay* (Ramesh Sippy, 1975).

he says, insouciantly: *Veeru se takkar?* (Taking Veeru on? What were you thinking?). There's a moment where the backfiring of a train is used in the place of a shot, the shot that will...but what am I thinking? If you haven't seen *Sholay*, I can't spoil that for you. Trains bring Jai and Veeru to Ramgarh. They take two away but not the same two. The lyrics conjure up trains: *Tayshun se gaadi jab chhoot jaati hai to ek do teen ho jaati hai* (When a train leaves the station, well then, it leaves the station). Uhm. This is not the most foolish line from a Hindi film song involving trains. That must go to *Mome ki Gudiya* (Mohan Kumar, 1972), where in a cabaret, Helen mouths the immortal lines: *Nainon ki gaadi chali, gaadi chali chhuk-chhuk-chhuk-chhuk* (The train of eyes has begun to move, chhuk-chhuk-chhuk-chhuk).

Is Amitabh Bachchan the train man then? He was a *Coolie* (Manmohan Desai, 1983), it should be remembered, and carried *saari duniya ka bojh*, the weight of the world. He cavorted on a train roof, too, in the song, *Accident ho gaya, agreement ho gaya, permanent ho gaya*, but then who hasn't? There was Rishi Kapoor and Padmini Kolhapure in *Hoga tumse pyaara kaun?* (Who could be more loveable?) in *Zamaane ko Dikhaana hai* (Nasir Hussain, 1981) and Shah Rukh Khan and Malaika Arora in *Chaiyya-Chaiyya* in *Dil Se* (Mani Ratnam, 1998). Most other actors preferred to stay inside the train and who could blame them? Dev Anand told us that his heart was a wanderer in *Solva Saal* (Raj Khosla, 1958) and sang *Phoolon ke rang se* in *Prem Pujari* (Dev Anand, 1970) to a group of bemused pink persons. (This was before a lake in Switzerland was named after Yash Chopra, way back in the day when international shoots were the exception rather than the norm.) Finally, there is *Gaadi bulaa rahi hai, seeti bajaa rahi hai, chalna hi zindagi hai, chalti hi jaa rahi hai* (The train calls, the whistle sounds, to move is life, and it will not stop moving) from *Dost* (Dulal Guha, 1974).

Oddly enough, there was no train song in *Chennai Express* (Rohit Shetty, 2013) although once again the idea of the train as a place of romance and of encounter was exploited to the hilt. Shah Rukh Khan plays yet another Rahul and yet again, we were brought into a close encounter with *Dilwale Dulhaniya Le Jayenge*—is this some kind of lucky charm—as the forty-year-old hero sets off with the ashes of his grandfather. He wants to cheat his destiny and go off to Goa; the heroine and her predicament take him into the deep south where on a railway bridge, two streams meet and cascade into a waterfall.

This then is the secret of our fascination with trains. They were our road movies, our rail movies. You could read growth on to them, you could turn the journey into a series of vignettes. You could board with a *Half-Ticket* (Kalidas, 1962) and a pocket full of contraband as Kishore Kumar did; or you could ride a magnificent train engine and go forth from your small town, bored of the narrow horizons and the dust, ready to take on the world by fair means or foul as Abhishek Bachchan and Rani Mukherjee do in *Bunty aur Babli* (Shaad Ali, 2005). The trains keep going, the films keep rolling, and we watch in fascination as our lives play out on the parallel tracks that meet somewhere in the distance, somewhere out at infinity.

RAILWAYS: A 160-YEAR HERITAGE

Gillian Wright

It is difficult to believe that anyone who has ever been a passenger on Indian Railways could have failed to be touched by its magnificent and almost omnipresent heritage. Indeed, could anyone who has even driven past historic stations like the Chhatrapati Shivaji Terminus—formerly Victoria Terminus—in Mumbai, have failed to be impressed by its architectural exuberance, it's ability to outshine London's St. Pancras station? Across the land, even the humblest branch line stations with their rows of thick-boled shade trees along the length of the platforms, have their history as well as immense charm. And then, there are the half-timbered cottage stations of India's narrow gauge hill

> It is difficult to believe that anyone who has ever been a passenger on Indian Railways could have failed to be touched by its magnificent and almost omnipresent heritage.

railways and the varied architecture—from Rajput to Nawabi—of the railways of India's erstwhile princely states. Heritage bridges and tunnels, although adapted for modern needs, still connect India. Among them, the Pamban Sea-bridge, officially the Annai Indira Gandhi Bridge, for many decades was the only way, except by boat, to reach the pilgrimage centre of Rameshwaram in southern India from the mainland.

In such a limited space one can only provide glimpses of the immense richness of the heritage of Indian railways. From 16 April 1853, when the first passenger service ran between Bombay, now Mumbai, and Thane, all kinds of government-owned, government-guaranteed, princely and private railways abounded. Their names resound to this day—the Great Indian Peninsula Railway, the Bombay-Baroda and Central Indian Railway, the East India Railway, the Bengal-Nagpur Railway and the Madras and Southern Mahratta Railway to name but a few. During the reorganization of railways in 1951, these different railways were integrated into independent India's state-owned and-run railway system, the present custodian of the country's rail heritage.

In my experience though, it is not so much the lines and their infrastructure that symbolize railway heritage for the general public. For them pride of place must surely go to the 'chug-chug gaari'— the steam locomotive. The older of you reading this article will remember, as I do, the last years of steam, and will have their own special memories. I recall in particular the great WP Class locomotives eking out their last days as shunting engines at Hazrat Nizamuddin station, the glorious sight of the round engine shed at Moradabad, which gradually emptied of its steam locomotives, and the night-time turntable at Kanchipuram, when locomotives slowly revolved, their fireboxes glowing. I still remember with a thrill of excitement the occasion I was lucky enough to travel on the footplate of steam service from Jodhpur to Jaisalmer (then metre gauge) as the sun rose over the desert.

However, heritage is not just about nostalgia, or about the aesthetics and intrinsic appeal of the machines and buildings of yesteryear. As the late Mike Satow, the indefatigable engineer and railway historian, who was the moving spirit behind the creation of the National Railway Museum, put it: 'One often hears the question, "What is the use of preserving it—it belongs to the past?" There can be no future without a past and our teaching of today is based on the learning from the past… The railways played a significant part in the development of communications and trade, a part which is clearly definable.'

Mike Satow lived and breathed railways, and he devoted over two decades of his life to the creation of the National Railway Museum. Mike's involvement began in 1970 when he happened to visit the transport museum at Clapham in London and was asked by the curator if he could help in moving an ornate railway coach, built in Lucknow in 1870, back to India for a proposed new museum. Mike happily agreed and the very same year accepted the position that he was to hold for so many years—as Honorary Advisor to the Ministry of Railways. Under his guidance the museum took shape, the foundation stone being laid at the site in the leafy diplomatic enclave of Chanakyapuri by then President of India, V.V. Giri, in 1971. Mike then devoted years to searching for exhibits, in particular steam locomotives, and took immense delight in working with the railways' engineers to bring them back to life.

One of the most dramatic examples of this was an obscure Punjab railway. Taking a lead from a 1964 article by a Mr Ambler in *Railway World* magazine, Mike learned of and began to research a monorail system that operated from Patiala and Sunam between 1907 and 1914. This was hauled by four remarkable locomotives with outrigger wheels to balance them. Mike finally found the remains of the four locomotives and carriages half buried in a PWD scrap yard in Patiala, understandably in an appallingly decrepit state. He managed to get permission for the best of them to be moved to the Railway Workshop at Amritsar, and was closely involved with restoring them to working condition.

Especially close to the hearts of all of those associated with the museum is the Fairy Queen, acknowledged by the Guinness Book of Records to be the oldest working steam engine in the world and by the Indian government to be a national treasure.

Bought by the East India Railway (EIR) in 1855, she belongs to the same class of locomotive that pulled the first passenger train to leave Calcutta's Howrah station on 15 August 1854. Manufactured by Kitson Thompson and Hewitson of Leeds in England, she was built for the broad gauge and has a wheel arrangement of 2-2-2 with an underslung water tank and weight of twenty-six tons. Her original EIR number was 22, after which she was renumbered twice and finally given her name in 1895, after forty years of service. Although originally used for hauling light mail trains between Howrah and Raniganj, covering 195 kms in five hours, she ended her working life in Bihar in 1909. From then until 1943 she was placed on a pedestal outside Howrah station before being moved to the Zonal Training School, Chandausi, where she remained until 1972, when under Mike's guidance she was brought to the Railway Museum.

The Fairy Queen has since travelled well beyond the limits of the museum, making her first long run since retirement in 1997. I had the pleasure of travelling from Delhi Cantonment to Alwar on one of her regular outings. Passengers would take great delight in reaching the Cantonment station well in advance of the train's departure to spend time with the engine in all her glory, her black and green livery polished mirror-bright and her interior with its shiny brass fittings. Tragically, in 2011, vandals robbed her of practically all her removable parts, including her rhythmic whistle.

These could not be recovered but the railways rose to the challenge. Replicas of the missing parts were manufactured in the Perambur Loco Workshop in Chennai where she was moved for repair. Today, the grand old lady of Indian Railways is back in shape, although for the time being a WP Class locomotive is taking her place on the bi-monthly steam run between Delhi and Alwar.

Mike Satow and his colleagues would be proud to know that later generations of railwaymen and women would continue to cherish the national museum. On a recent visit, I found that the Patiala monorail had again been revived and run after several years out of service. One of the first Darjeeling Himalayan Railway engines had just been restored to its original green livery, and work was underway to restore railcars and rolling stock of the Kalka-Shimla and Matheran hill railways. The director had just driven the magnificent red Morris fire engine—belonging to the Nizam's State Railway—in a vintage car rally, and could personally vouch for its continued roadworthiness. However, like all committed heritage men, he knew there was much more work to be done. Many of the original outdoor exhibits, for example, needed care and attention.

Conservation of railway heritage demands long-term commitment. And the Rewari Loco Shed, now known as the Mecca of Indian steam, is an example of this commitment. Rewari was, in a way, an obvious location for a heritage shed. Not only is it a comfortable two-hour journey from Delhi and well connected by road, it has a long history as an important junction on the metre gauge of the old BB&CI Railway. In his voluminous handwritten Minute of 1853 that charted the future of Indian Railways, the then Governor-General, Lord Dalhousie, had envisaged a single gauge for the whole of India. However, this was not to be. The broad gauge of five-foot-six-inches was expensive, and to minimize costs it was argued that lighter gauges should also be used. This suggestion found favour with the Viceroy Lord Mayo, who remarked, 'When we have an elephant's load, we may use an elephant, but when we have only a donkey's load we have to use a donkey'. As a result, at the time of Independence, India had 24,000 kms of broad gauge, 16,000 kms of metre gauge and 2,200 kms of narrow gauge lines, and has since then embarked on a major programme known as uni-gauging so that India's rail network can be truly integrated.

Rewari, now converted to broad gauge, had the largest metre gauge loco shed of the BB&CI, employing at its height some five hundred maintenance staff. Even in the early 1980s, it housed sixty-five metre gauge locomotives, and was a major crew depot. With the replacement of steam, the loco shed was closed in 1993 with all but two of its locomotives cut up and sold as scrap. For a few years, diesel locomotives were maintained here but Rewari again saw steam in 1994 with the running of the Royal Orient Express from Delhi. From the turn of the twenty-first century there emerged plans to make the loco shed a heritage attraction, and part of it was converted to broad gauge in preparation for this. Two WP Class locomotives were sent to the shed in 2002, but somewhere along the way this project lost steam and in February 2010, the shed's twenty-five engineers, or 'old steam guys', took it upon themselves to work wonders. Within the year, the absent locomotives were hauled back to Delhi, and all the shed's locomotives nursed back to health and steamed up. The shed itself was repaired and vintage artifacts collected for exhibition at a new museum.

The Rewari shed today holds a treasure trove of historic working locomotives. Among them are the two WP Class locomotives, giants of the broad gauge, their bull-noses marked with a silver star. These WP steam locomotives were introduced after the Second World War for passenger duties, marking the change from 'X' to 'W' as the classification code for broad gauge locomotives. The older of the two, WP 7200, was one of the first

Lucknow's Charbagh Railway Station.

Mumbai's Chhatrapati Shivaji Terminus, formerly known as Victoria Terminus (1979).

An old photograph of Delhi Junction.

Howrah railway station (1906).

Churchgate railway station (1876).

Asansol railway station.

Bikaner railway station.

A view of a tunnel from another tunnel on the Kalka–Shimla Railway.

2nd Ramganga Bridge, Moradabad (1970).

Class 4-6-2 103 (VF 1939) 'Silver Arrow' engine operated by the North Western Railway (1947).

A passenger train of the Bombay, Baroda and Central India Railway.

prototypes of this class to be ordered from the Baldwin Locomotive Works in Philadelphia, USA, to cope with a severe shortage of locomotives in the 1940s. They quickly became the standard broad gauge passenger locomotives, known for their 'free steaming, fuel economy and good riding characteristics'. The WP 7200 is believed not only to have been the first WP prototype handed over to the Indian Railways, but also to have been handed over on 15 August 1947—Independence Day. For this reason the loco bears the name 'Azaad', meaning 'Free'. The second WP Class loco, called 'Akbar' after the great Mughal emperor, was built at the Chittaranjan Locomotive Works in West Bengal in 1965. 'Akbar' spent its work life based at the Saharanpur shed of Northern Railway, also the last home of 'Azaad' before retirement.

There is only one surviving XE (X Eagle) Class locomotive that can be put to steam and this is 'Angadh', named after one of the great monkey warriors of the *Ramayana*. It was built in Britain in 1930 and was operated by the Madhya Pradesh Electricity Board in their Kobra Thermal Power Plant where it hauled coal. The XE Class was the largest unarticulated steam locomotive ever used on Indian Railways, standing fourteen-feet-eight-inches tall and weighing 200 tons.

The most powerful locomotive class ever to run on Indian Railways—the AWE Class (Baldwin variant of XE)—was another of the imports made during the Second World War. The one at Rewari is aptly named 'Virat' or 'Majestic'. 'Virat' was built in 1943, and is one of the oldest locomotives of its class. These were based mainly at Bhusawal and Ratlam and their enormous strength was put to full use on the ghat or hill sections of central and western India.

Rewari also preserves 'Sher-e-Punjab', the 'Lion of Punjab', the WL Class locomotive that hauled the last broad gauge steam passenger train on the Indian Railways system—train No. 4JF between Firozpur and Jalandhar on 6 December 1995. 'Sher-e-

Punjab' was one of the first ten WL Class locomotives ever to be made. These were manufactured in Britain in the Vulcan Foundary in 1955. Between 1966 and 1968, ninety-four more locomotives of this class, designed to work on lighter branch lines, were built in India at the Chittaranjan Loco Works. This particular locomotive started its career with Southern Railway before being brought up to Punjab.

It has to be said that there was an entirely different pleasure in travelling on the metre gauge, a charm in the smaller dimension of the engines and the carriages, a different kind of motion to experience. Rewari has one metre gauge passenger locomotive of the YP Class, 'Rewari King', to illustrate this and three goods locomotives of the YG Class, 'Sahib', 'Sultan' and 'Sindh', named after the three steam locomotives that hauled the first-ever passenger train in India in 1853. YPs were adapted Baldwins ordered for the Jodhpur MG network in 1948; some were later built in India. YGs were also imported at first (some from Germany; others were Baldwins) but later built in India by CLW and Telco.

Most of the Indian Railways' tangible heritage is, of course, not to be found in museums but in regular daily use by the general public and by the railways' employees. The most magnificent of the many heritage stations is Chhatrapati Shivaji Terminus, originally Victoria Terminus and still referred to affectionately as VT. Now on UNESCO's World Heritage list, it's one of India's most iconic buildings. When the makers of the Hindi blockbuster *Ra-One* wanted a runaway train to spectacularly crash through a station wall as the climax of their movie, they naturally chose VT as the location—the crash was, of course, computer-simulated.

Opened on Queen Victoria's Jubilee in 1887, VT originally served the dual purpose of headquarters and main terminus of the Great Indian Peninsula Railway (GIP). The architect, FW Stevens

(1848-1900), used all his imagination to create a building that was ornate and awe-inspiring in its scale. He drew his inspiration from the Venetian Gothic style blended with Indian elements. Roughly in the shape of a C enclosing a courtyard opening on to the street, VT's ground plan has also been compared to traditional Indian palace architecture. The terminus' arches, turrets, spires and smaller domes culminate in one great dome of dove-tailed ribs surmounted by a statue of a woman, symbolizing progress and holding a torch in one hand, and a wheel in the other. The main construction is of Indian lime- and sandstone, with a riot of foliage and other carvings, including gargoyles and hemispherical jaalis of peacocks. The interiors are lavishly decorated with stained glass, wrought iron, brasswork, glazed tiles and polished Aberdeen granite columns, and the ground floor of the North Wing—still the booking office—is embellished with Italian marble. Surmounting the entrance gates are statues of the British lion and the Indian tiger.

The BB&CI Railway did not want to be outdone by the GIP. Therefore, when it decided to build its headquarters in central Bombay, it took VT as a model and employed the same architect. The result—the second great Victorian High Gothic railway building in Bombay. Built at Churchgate between 1894 and 1899, it is now the headquarters of Western Railway. Three storeys high and clad in Indian blue basalt stone with contrasting Porbandar and Dhragaddra red stone in its many arches, it has a remarkable square central tower 100 feet high, topped by an octagonal section and a dome. Unfortunately, illuminations put up to celebrate the visit to Bombay of the Prince and Princess of Wales in 1905, set the building on fire. As FW Stevens was no longer alive, the BB&CI called on his son, Charles, to supervise repairs to its badly damaged interiors, including expanses of Burma teak,

Charles Stevens was also the architect of the premier training institution for officers of the Indian Railways—the Railway Staff

College at Vadodara, formerly Baroda. However, this was not a building designed for the railways but for the ruling family of the princely state of Baroda. They chose to have a palace in classic Renaissance revival style, a departure from the High Indo-Saracenic Gothic of Bombay. Designed in 1900, completed in 1914 and handed over to the railways in 1950, this erstwhile palace is surmounted by a central copper dome, and there is a stunning grandeur to the restrained columns and tall windows of its façade. Inside, young railway officers now have the privilege of climbing its regal marble staircase. The Staff College is not the only major heritage building of Baroda State to be used by the modern railways. The Northern Railway headquarters in Delhi is housed in the elegant Baroda House, situated at the foot of the central vista that stretches from Rashtrapati Bhavan, the Presidential Palace, down Rajpath to the India Gate war memorial.

The pattern of grand stations and railway headquarters was repeated in the major cities of India in different styles. Even within Bombay itself, there was a notable variety of architecture, and surely there can be no greater contrast to VT's ornateness than the simplicity of the exterior of Bombay Central Station, built in 1930. As the late RR Bhandari, the indefatigable chronicler of Indian Railways wrote, 'It was the most modern building of its kind in India at that point of time, with wide approaches, the main façade, well away from the road, impressively set off by a massive 65-foot concrete arch and a wide portico of equal length'.

In Calcutta, now Kolkata, the first city of the British Empire, the principal station was built for economic reasons in Howrah on the opposite bank of the Hooghly river to Calcutta and the headquarters of the East Indian Railway (EIR) in Fairlie Place. As the historian Sukanta Chaudhuri put it, 'It was the railway that first raised Haora (sic) above the status of a small village. The main booking office was on the Calcutta bank, at the Armenian Ghat, and the fare covered the ferry to the station'. The first Howrah station, the terminus of the EIR, was no more than a tin shed and a single track. The need for a suitably impressive station was met when the present one was designed by Halsey Ricardo and built in Romanesque style between 1901 and 1906. Standing, as it does, on the banks of the river, no other buildings could veil its imposing red brick façade, but passengers continued to complain about the inconvenience of reaching it. A pontoon bridge failed to end their woes and it was not until 1943 that the New Howrah Bridge was finally commissioned. A cantilever bridge with a suspended span, when it was built was the third longest bridge of its type in the world. Constructed mainly of Tata Steel it was assembled in four different yards in Calcutta. The Howrah Bridge became one of the great symbols of that city, and in 1965 was renamed the Rabindra Setu after Nobel laureate Rabindranath Tagore. However, it never managed to provide a lasting solution to the problems of traffic congestion between the station and the city centre.

Garden Reach is another riverside area of Kolkata rich in railway heritage. Once the site of the palaces of the Raj, it then became home to the Nawab of Avadh, Wajid Ali Shah, in his years of exile—from the time his kingdom was annexed in 1856 until his death. In 1908, the Bengal-Nagpur Railway opened its headquarters here. Designed by the architect V.J. Esch, the monumental building is constructed mainly in red brick with contrasting white details and domes. Now the headquarters of the South-Eastern Railway, it has a square plan with large central quadrangles to make the best use of the river breezes. All the rooms are open on both sides and most have good natural light.

Chennai (formerly Madras) Central station, the city's principal railway terminus, opened in 1868 and is another interpretation of Romanesque revival style, with much deeper roofs than Howrah, and avoiding ornamentation. In contrast, Chennai's

Egmore station, designed by E.C. Bird and built by the Bengaluru contractor, T. Samynada Pillai, that opened forty years later, is profoundly Indo-Saracenic in style, with a most attractive white Bengal-hut pavilion decorating the main portico. Both these stations have been adapted for modern times. Egmore has been converted from a metre to a broad gauge station, and Central has been considerably enlarged to add more platforms. After Egmore, the contractor T. Samynada Pillai went on to construct another of Chennai's landmarks combining European and Indian elements— the grand twin towered headquarters of the Madras and Southern Mahratta Railway, now Southern Railway.

Throughout the subcontinent, princely states were quick to finance and build their own railways, in some cases having to overcome the objections of certain British officials. In the south there was the Nizam's State Railway, in the west the Kathiawar Railway and the railways of the Gaekwad of Baroda, and Jodhpur-Bikaner Railway, to name just a few. The stations on these lines are built in the distinctive styles of their regions. Morbi station in Gujarat is considered one of the best examples of the Saurashtra style, while Bikaner is one of the finest of the many Rajput style stations. Even the British Indian Railways made efforts to relate to traditions of local architecture. For example, Lucknow's Charbagh, opened in 1926, echoes Indian design with its tiers of rather severe chhatris and its recessed arches.

Charbagh's location, to the south of the old city and within easy reach of the army cantonment, also bears testament to British concerns after the First War of Independence or Great Revolt of 1857. Fearing another uprising, they constructed stations in places that allowed swift troop movements or as defensible positions. Built in 1864 and opened to the public in 1903, the grand red brick Delhi Junction station building even resembles a castle with its six crenalated turrets that doubled as water tanks. Constructed the same year, Lahore station, now in Pakistan, appears even more of a fortress with loop-holes to fire muskets and bomb-proof towers.

Another railway building in Delhi—which now houses the Construction Office of Northern Railway—has a much more direct association with the Revolt. Built in 1803 in the historic Kashmiri Gate area of Old Delhi, this domed bungalow with round windows and a triple arched entrance, served as a prison for the last Mughal emperor, Bahadur Shah Zafar, after his defeat.

Heritage buildings across India include the townships, housing colonies, bungalows, clubs and institutes where railway employees and their families lived and entertained themselves and continue to do so to this day. To work on the railway was to be part of a community, and employees were cared for in sickness and in health. To this day a hundred railway hospitals—many with a considerable history—and their 50,000 medical staff tend to the 1.4 million employees. The Jackson Hospital in Dahod is one such heritage hospital that continues a tradition of service that began in 1930 when it was inaugurated by Lady Jackson, wife of Sir Earnest Jackson, then the Agent of the BB&CI in Bombay. This spotless hospital roofed with Mangalore tiles that shade its verandahs has the atmosphere of a cottage hospital while offering the most modern treatment.

Railway workshops were among the institutions with their own complete townships. Jamalpur, seven kilometres south of the River Ganga in Munger district of Bihar in eastern India, was the first to be opened in 1862 as the main workshop of the EIR.

Since the early years Jamalpur has expanded vastly and prides itself on being not just the oldest, but the biggest and most diversified workshop of the Indian Railways' 700 repair shops. It now produces wagons, jacks and cranes and repairs diesel locomotives and a wide range of other equipment. The original technical school has developed through various incarnations, until today it is the prestigious Indian Railways Institute of Mechanical and Electrical Engineering (IRIMEE), renowned for its academic excellence.

Above all, the creation of the Indian Railways was an extraordinary feat of engineering. As rail historian Ian J. Kerr put it, 'construction was the heroic and most compelling story in the early decades'. V. Nilakant and S. Ramnarayan in their remarkable account of Indian Railways, *Changing Tracks*, say, 'It was one of the most astonishing feats of human endeavour. Although it was planned, managed and directed by the British, millions of Indians working as labourers built the railway lines, stations, tunnels and bridges... Many of them, including some of the British, succumbed to disease and accidents during construction.' Nilakant and Ramnarayan also make the important point that railway engineers in India led the world in many aspects of civil engineering, in particular in controlling or training rivers that flowed beneath bridges. These railway bridge-builders had to be innovators and they had to be prepared to learn from local wisdom. They had to deal with tidal rivers such as the Hooghly, and rivers that shrank in the dry season to a trickle and transformed into roaring torrents in the monsoon; they had to cope with different kinds of subsoil, and they had to bridge mountain ravines. They did so with various techniques, using stone piers, steel girders, masonry arches and, on the Kangra Valley Railway, a steel arch. The bridges and tunnels of India's heritage hill railways are, however, considered in detail in another chapter, so I will say no more here.

With all this engineering prowess, it's ironic that of all the 120,000 railway bridges on modern India's network, the oldest, and possibly the oldest in the world, was not constructed by railway engineers. This viaduct of tall, narrow arches crosses the Kabini river in Karnataka near Nanjangud station. It was built around 1735, well over a century before the first historic steam run, by Dalvoy Devaraj and served as a road bridge for bullock carts and the like through the reigns of Haider Ali and Tipu Sultan of Mysore, to the days of the Raj. It became a railway bridge in 1902 when a metre gauge line was laid across it and it remained in daily use for over a hundred years until the line was converted to broad gauge and a new bridge was constructed. Today it is a tourist attraction.

The oldest purpose-built railway bridge, constructed in 1854, is the Dapoorie Viaduct, twenty-eight arches that link Bombay Island to the mainland of Thane. This was followed by numerous wide-span girder bridges that crossed India's major rivers, many of which also accommodated road traffic. In 1863, the first bridge over the Son river on the route between Calcutta and Delhi was completed, followed in 1865 by the Yamuna Bridge at Allahabad, and the next year by the bridge over the Yamuna in Delhi passing between the Red Fort and the fort of Salimgarh. In 1887, the Dufferin Bridge, later renamed the Malaviya Bridge, was opened at Varanasi, complete with military-style block houses at each end, and in the same year the first railway bridge over the Hooghly, the Jubilee Bridge north of Calcutta, was inaugurated. The Upper Son Bridge, or Nehru Sethu, opened in 1900, was until recently the longest railway bridge in India. Serving the shorter Calcutta-Delhi route, known as the Grand Chord, it is 3,064-metre long. Bridge No. 493, historically known as the 'Arch Gallery', situated between Kandaghat and Kanoh stations on the Kalka-Shimla track, is an arch bridge in three stages, constructed with stone masonry that stands good even today.

Perhaps the most dramatic of heritage bridges, though, is India's first and only rail sea-bridge, mentioned earlier, linking the temple town of Rameshwaram on Pamban Island with the mainland of southeastern India. It stands in a place forever

> Perhaps the most dramatic of heritage bridges, though, is India's first and only rail sea-bridge, mentioned earlier, linking the temple town of Rameshwaram on Pamban Island with the mainland of south-eastern India.

associated with Rama, the hero of the *Ramayana* epic, who crosses the sea to Lanka, the land of the demon-king Ravana, to rescue his abducted wife Sita. In the epic, Rama's army of monkey-warriors construct a bridge to make this possible. Traditionally, this bridge is identified with the shallow strait that is the closest point between the modern states of India and Sri Lanka, extending between Pamban Island and the Sri Lankan island of Mannar. Long fingers of land extend from each island towards each other across the sea.

The immediate spur for the sea-bridge, however, was not religious but commercial. From the 1900s, tea planters in Ceylon, as Sri Lanka was then known, were demanding a shorter, better link between the two countries. Various options were discussed, including taking a rail-link across the entire distance, but more modest counsels prevailed and a steamer service was chosen to cross the Palk Strait between Talaimannar on Mannar Island, and Dhanushkodi at the far end of Pamban Island. On the Indian side a viaduct was constructed from Mandapam on the mainland to the end of the narrow, sandy promontory of Tonturai Point, and from there a rail bridge 2,057 metres long was constructed on granite and cement piers built on a sandstone reef across the sea.

The route of this bridge crossed a shipping channel, which had to be kept open. Scherzer Rolling Lift Company of Chicago designed a two-leafed bridge which when raised would leave vessels a clear 200-foot passage, and this was built by Head, Wrightson and Co. of Thornaby-on-Tees in England. From the end of the bridge the line continued to Pamban station where it bifurcated—one branch proceeding to the town of Rameshwaram, and the other to Dhanushkodi. The Ceylon service from Madras opened on 24 February 1914 and the metre gauge 1Up/2 Down Ceylon Boat Mail ran from Chennai's Egmore to Dhanushkodi until 22 December 1964. That night a massive cyclone hit the coast. Waves submerged a passenger train near Dhanushkodi, killing all on board, destroying that branch of the line, and washing away most of the Pamban sea-bridge.

The Dhanushkodi line was abandoned, but in an astounding feat of salvage and engineering, the bridge's girders were recovered and reassembled in just two months. The bridge, always a challenge to maintain in an extremely corrosive and often stormy environment, underwent major alteration in 2007 when the railways completed conversion to the broad gauge—an exemplary illustration of heritage successfully maintained and modernized. In 2014 celebrations marked its centenary.

As I said at the start of this article, these are just a few glimpses of the wealth of India's rail heritage. The question that lies before the railways now, is how to utilize this wealth in a world where rail heritage awareness and tourism is growing fast. The railways have come a long way from the last days of steam when old locomotives were mostly seen as scrap metal. There is now a Heritage Committee in the railways and there are many achievements it can be proud of. But if the railways are serious and consistent there is potential for much more. I myself look forward to the day when rail heritage in India truly comes into its own and a journey on a steam-hauled train will be as essential a part of a holiday in India as a visit to the Taj.

THE SPIRIT OF THE RAILWAYS

Biswadeep Ghosh

The Indian Railways unites India in more ways than one. Its network of tracks criss-crossing the country not only brings different parts of India closer together, but also serves as a great social unifier. The railways have been a melting pot of cultures and traditions. The efficiency of the nation's most favoured form of transport is such that a lay traveller can be deluded into believing that monitoring and managing this giant is not difficult. This misconception can be attributed to the spirit of the Indian Railways, which enables it to surmount the challenges and obstacles day after day after day. Whether these obstacles are *rail roko* agitations, damages caused by disruptive elements or natural calamities, each roadblock is negotiated by the men and women of the Indian Railways with exemplary strategizing and resolve. With the ability to confront exigencies ingrained in its DNA, Indian Railways carries on, proudly, creating new benchmarks of performance for its counterparts in nations worldwide.

What makes this mammoth organization tick? Operating in a

> The Indian Railways carries more passengers than the entire population of Australia every day and operates tracks which are substantially larger than the circumference of the Earth...

country where it carries more passengers than the entire population of Australia every day and operates tracks which are substantially larger than the circumference of the Earth, even a stray incident in a tiny segment of its huge system can have a ripple effect on the functioning of the entire railway network. Large-scale man-made and natural turbulence are hazards that the system must deal with on a fairly regular basis. But it is the spirit of the 1.4 million employees of the Indian Railways which ensures that the disruption remains limited to the area where the incident takes place. In fact, it is their spirit that binds them together.

The ways to deal with some of the bigger challenges faced by the railways have been laid out by the Indian Railways in its Disaster Management Plan (DMP) 2009. According to the document, more than 40 million hectares (12 per cent of the land) of India's landmass is susceptible to floods and river erosion. Out of the 7,516-kilometre-long coastline, cyclones and tsunamis can disturb nearly 5,700 kilometres. Hilly areas experience landslides and avalanches, whereas drought impacts 68 per cent of the cultivable area.

In keeping with the definition of the Disaster Management Act 2005, the Ministry of Railways' DMP 2009 explains Railway Disaster thus: 'Railway Disaster is a serious train accident or an untoward event of grave nature, either on railway premises or arising out of railway activity, due to natural or man-made causes, that may lead to loss of many lives and/or grievous injuries to a large number of people, and/or severe disruption of traffic etc., necessitating large scale help from other Government/Non-government and Private Organizations.'

The Indian Railways has put in place an integrated approach to these problems. Furthermore, the Indian Railways Disaster Management Plan–2013 is extremely comprehensive and lays down the various steps that have to be taken in case of contingencies, such as cyclones, floods, earthquakes, landslides and snow avalanches, biological disasters, chemical disasters, and nuclear and radiological emergency (disasters).

But no amount of planning can prepare one for the kind of tragedy that happened in Mumbai on 26/11. It is during such moments of grave crises that stories of human courage rise above the debris that the tragedy leaves behind. Years after the cowardly attacks on Mumbai ripped through the soul of the city, everyone remembers the announcer whose bravery at the Chhatrapati Shivaji Terminus (CST) on that day saved the lives of hundreds of unsuspecting commuters.

Central Railway announcer Vishnu Zende's name might have been forgotten by most people, but what nobody will forget is his act of extreme bravery. Zende was on announcement duty on that day. When Bablu Kumar Deepak, another announcer on duty at the long distance terminal, saw Ajmal Amir Kasab hurl a grenade and open fire, he immediately informed both the chief announcer and Zende, who was on duty for local trains. Zende instinctively stepped into a role that had not been envisaged for him—that of a disaster management personnel.

While two terrorists, Abu Ismail and Kasab, went around the main hall of the local line section, firing indiscriminately and killing people, Zende continued to warn the travellers, asking them to evacuate the railway station. He also intimated the Government Railway Police (GRP) and the Railway Protection Force (RPF) so that they could act immediately. On hearing these announcements, the terrorists rushed to the control room to find the announcer. They opened fire on Zende, but luckily he escaped unhurt. But there were others who were equally brave but not as lucky. In his effort to inform the control room and assist the injured, Assistant Chief Ticket Inspector Sushil Kumar Sharma didn't survive the bullets which penetrated his lungs and shoulder. Senior Inspector of CST Government Railway Police, Shashank Shinde, and head constable of the Railway Protection Force, M.L. Chaudhary, also died in the shootout.

The aftermath of 26/11 paralyzed the financial capital for almost four days, but train services resumed within six hours of the attack after combing operations and the deployment of heavy security along the Central Railway line.

While 26/11 is among the worst experiences of a metropolis in recent times, Mumbai, especially its suburban railway network, has been a victim of terrorism on earlier occasions, too. In 2003, a bomb exploded inside a local train as it pulled into Mulund station, leading to the death of twelve people and injury to many others. Another horrific incident took place on 11 July 2006 when a series of seven explosions on local trains happened within a span of eleven minutes. Since the blasts occurred during peak travel hours—between 6.24 p.m. and 6.35 p.m.—it led to the loss of more than 200 lives and injury to well over 700 others.

So powerful were these explosions on the Western line of the suburban railway network that the walls of coaches blew up upon impact. In Mahim, some equipment that was inside a coach flew out and landed on the third floor of a building. These visuals would have stunned the average person, but not the railway employees for whom helping the injured, informing the relatives of the dead who had been identified, and resuming services had to be prioritized.

The explosions might have shattered some carriages, but they failed to shatter the morale of the employees. Western Railway resumed its services by 10 p.m. with a few trains starting from Churchgate going to Bandra and then to Andheri. After the mangled coaches were cleared up, the network became fully functional by 10 a.m. the next day. Mumbai was on the move once again.

The sight of moving trains is a reassuring one for Mumbaikars. Those who run the Mumbai locals realize what these trains mean to the city's inhabitants. That's the reason why, after every such attack, the railways focus on restoring normal operations with exemplary fortitude. The city's population that is hugely reliant on them starts boarding them in the belief that the worst is over and normalcy has returned.

> The sight of moving trains is a reassuring one for Mumbaikars. Those who run the Mumbai locals realize what these trains mean to the city's inhabitants.

The same spirit unites all Railway employees, no matter where they serve. The stories of courage and conviction are no different along the Red Corridor, a territory notorious for Maoist insurgency. Comprising Bihar, Chhattisgarh, Jharkhand, Madhya Pradesh, Andhra Pradesh, Odisha, Uttar Pradesh and West Bengal, this region, too, has experienced disruptive activity from time to time.

Among the more haunting memories is the derailment of Eastern Railway's Rajdhani Express over the Dhawa river near the town of Rafiganj near Gaya on the night of 10 September 2002. The train was headed towards New Delhi from Howrah with around 1,000 people on board, and the accident occurred at 10.40 p.m., nearly six hours after the train had left Howrah. Fifteen out of the eighteen coaches derailed, with two plunging into the river. Although the Maoists didn't claim responsibility for the attack, the media widely reported that they were responsible for the derailment which was supposed to have been caused by removing fishplates.

The derailment of Howrah-Kurla Jnaneswari Super Deluxe Express on 28 May 2010 killed more than 140 passengers. Another tragedy of massive proportions, it took place around seven kilometres away from Khemashuli station in West Bengal. Later, it was found that 46 centimetres of railway track had been removed, indicating sabotage. *The Hindu* reported that after the incident had occurred, the Director General of Police Bhupinder Singh said that the Maoists and the Maoist-backed organizations had orchestrated this disaster that had claimed numerous lives. This seemed plausible, the derailment having taken place less than a couple of hours after the Maoists had declared a bandh in the region.

Running trains through such a sensitive territory on a regular basis and working in them in different assigned roles must be a psychologically challenging experience. However, train-related tragedies do not play upon the minds of railway employees since passengers and goods need to reach their respective destinations. Whether or not the train passes through the Red Corridor, the job must be done. What must be remembered, however, is that trains travelling through the Red Corridor are not the only ones to be targeted.

The ugly face of mankind's depravity has made other appearances: the Kurnool train crash of 2002 which killed twenty people; and the West Bengal rail disaster of 2006 in which five people died in the explosion. It is the spirit of the Indian Railways' employees that enables them to deal with such catastrophic tragedies. This spirit is born out of the awareness that the entire nation is dependent on trains day after day, all through the year. The system cannot afford to take an off on a national holiday. It has to assist and support a country as large as ours.

Disruptions of diverse kinds must be confronted and dealt with. Unpredictable 'rail roko' agitations can take place simply because groups of angry locals stop the train to protest against irregular water or electricity supply in their areas. Railway authorities have to find ways to tackle such obstacles lest the movement of trains gets affected for a long period. They might endeavour to persuade the protestors to abandon their agitation, but if the situation spins out of control, coordinating with the local administration becomes a necessity. Every such train has passengers who need to reach their destination on time. Some have to meet ailing elders at home; others might be rushing to a larger city for medical treatment; while there are those who must report on time for a job interview. The wheels can stop, but not for long, the train being the lifeline for such a large section of Indian society.

But not all such agitations take place because of minor issues like irregular water supply; in fact, more often than not, its antithesis is the reality that the Indian Railways must face. Political movements with thousands of supporters can paralyze the movement of trains. When these take place, several trains need to be rescheduled and diverted in a sustained effort to keep the system running and diminish the degree of inconvenience to the passengers in every possible way.

In India, 'rail roko' agitations have become a favoured form of protest. Why it is so isn't difficult to understand. Unlike the airlines, the railways is not a closed system. Trains move through exposed territories, with tracks laid on the ground under the skies. Conducting protests in and around the tracks—and very often, after occupying them—is an easy way to manifest one's simmering discontent for various reasons. Historically, the railway authorities have had to accept such impediments as part of their jobs. Agitations with millions of supporters are particularly hindersome, and overcoming them, anything but simple.

In such cases, the authorities have to resort to traditional methods of dealing with the problem such as cancelling, rescheduling and diverting trains. The passengers might be inconvenienced for a while but gradually, the trains begin their journeys with the discipline they once did. This is a victory for a system that resists, fights and doesn't give up.

The nation falls back on the services of the Indian Railways during crises precipitated by nature. Everyone remembers with horror the 2002 Indian Ocean earthquake which had its epicentre off the west coast of Sumatra in Indonesia. The undersea megathrust earthquake had such an enormous impact that it resulted in many devastating tsunamis. According to a National Geographic report, the United States Geological Survey estimated that the occurence released as much energy as 23,000 atomic bombs dropped on Hiroshima would have. Indonesia was the worst affected. Other countries that bore the brunt were Sri Lanka, India and Thailand. In India, the tsunami affected the Andaman and Nicobar Islands, Kerala, Tamil Nadu, Andhra Pradesh and Pondicherry. All employees of the Indian Railways contributed one day's salary to the Prime Minister's Relief Fund. Trains carried all relief provisions for tsunami victims free of cost.

In June 2013, nature unleashed its fury in Uttarakhand, a young Indian state which is home to several significant pilgrimage sites, when a massive cloudburst caused landslides and floods. Nearly 6,000 people died, property wiped off the face of the earth and tourists and pilgrims trapped in several places.

Although regular railway services were disrupted, Indian Railways stepped into another role: that of the rescuer whose solitary mission was to evacuate stranded travellers who were in desperate need of help. Special relief trains were introduced, and affected passengers allowed to travel free of cost. Relief material was carried by trains from stations all over India to any station in Uttarakhand. Officers camping at Dehradun, Haridwar and Rishikesh stations coordinated with the state government authorities for systematic dispersal of passengers.

Unthinkable damage, the aftermath of any colossal disaster, cannot be erased overnight. But Indian Railways and its employees know that if and when another such disaster occurs, they will rise to the occasion and provide a compassionate helping hand to the hapless.

Railway employees have to deal with numerous day-to-day problems. A troublemaker may throw a stone and break a signal without being aware of the repercussions of his action. Or it could be a problem as as destructive as the Mumbai serial blasts of 2006. Or the Gujarat earthquake of 2001, where a sixty-kilometre-long railway track was being converted from metre gauge to broad gauge. Three days before its inauguration on 29 January, the earthquake struck, putting paid to all such plans. The railway station at Bhachau collapsed, yet employees worked day and night to ensure that the metre and broad gauge lines were functional within four days. The system suffered many other reversals due to the magnitude of the earthquake. But slowly, it was back on track.

The Indian Railways has evolved a very good support system for responding to emergencies. For instance, the Accident Relief Medical Equipment Train (ARME) has a response time of twenty minutes from the originating station to the accident spot. There is also the Accident Relief Train (ART), stationed at important locations and carrying equipment that can repair tracks and coaches, which has a response time of forty minutes. Such trains must move towards the site even though the information they receive is sketchy, but if, while en route, they receive the news that they are not required, they return to where they are stationed.

To say that the operations of the Indian Railways present challenges would be an understatement. Yet, the system despite its

> A lot of meticulous work goes into making train journeys safe and secure.

huge network functions remarkably well. It has suffered many damages, some inflicted by nature over which man has no control, others by certain people who deify the philosophy of destruction. There are setbacks in which tracks are destroyed, trains attacked, people die, and the well-defined pattern of operations goes awry for a while. But the institution soars above the impact of the tragedy, mainly because of the quick reactions from its employees at all levels. The planning by the superior officers is excellent, and coordination among zonal railways, various ministries and departments exemplary. Junior employees display single-minded dedication while performing their assigned roles. When normalcy returns, it is not a surprise; on the contrary, normalcy is just one more fulfilment of expectations that the people have from this system.

But very few citizens realize the dedication and hard work that makes this system work. Every minute, every inch of India's railway track is checked by a railway 'key man' who, regardless of extremities of weather or time of the day, physically checks the tracks for fractures, loose fish plates or any other problem. Personal safety is simply not a concern for them. Another example of this spirit can be seen among the staff working in railway yards and stations. They have lost limbs while working to ensure that the trains and coaches are safe for travel. This happens because of the constant movement of trains or 'light engines' or shunting engines, when the employee might fail to distinguish the warning whistle of an approaching engine of another train on perhaps a parallel track.

A lot of meticulous work goes into making train journeys safe and secure. Indian Railways has adopted many security measures, which includes installation of x-ray machines and scanners at railways stations, increasing the presence of security personnel on trains, and making use of trained dogs to check for explosives.

Despite continuous endeavours to improve security measures, the railways continue to face numerous occupational challenges. Railway stations being extremely porous, it is difficult to have any security apparatus at every entry point. Another problem is that the number of people who travel by rail is astounding, which makes the physical checking of passengers practically impossible.

Where will this institution go from here? Like all systems that epitomize consistently good performance down the years, it can only get better. Better use of technology, more trains for better connectivity, if we see a lot now, we are destined to see even more. Further improvement in the system will mean a better quality of life for the common man whom the Indian Railways has been servicing for well over one-and-a-half centuries.

> The spirit of the Indian Railways that has conquered impediments and grown stronger will ensure that it goes places.

The spirit of the Indian Railways that has conquered impediments and grown stronger will ensure that it goes places.

A glorious journey that began long ago will continue...

Select References

http://www.dnaindia.com/mumbai/report-2611-attacks-two-years-on-rail-announcer-vishnu-zende-has-moved-on-1471388

http://timesofindia.indiatimes.com/city/mumbai/Mulund-train-blast-toll-rises-to-12/articleshow/40189492.cms

http://edition.cnn.com/2006/WORLD/asiapcf/09/30/india.bombs

http://indiatoday.intoday.in/story/rajdhani-express-disaster-over-120-killed-safety-issues-in-indian-railways-loom-large/1/220926.html

http://epaper.timesofindia.com/Default/Scripting/ArticleWin.asp?From=Archive&Source=Page&Skin=TOINEW&BaseHref=TOIKM/2013/02/19&PageLabel=4&EntityId=Ar00402&ViewMode=HTML
http://www.thehindu.com/news/national/article440980.ece
http://channel.nationalgeographic.com/channel/episodes/asian-tsunami/
http://timesofindia.indiatimes.com/india/Railways-to-carry-relief-materials-free-of-cost-Lalu/articleshow/976255.cms?referral=PM

A points man setting the track in order to change the direction of an incoming train.

No adversity has ever stopped the Indian Railways from being an all weather transport system.

A stationmaster working under the light of a lamp in his cabin.

An old photograph showing a railway employee lighting a lamp at a railway station.

Construction of a railway tunnel on Kolkata's Metro Railway.

THE MAGIC OF HILL RAILWAYS

Gillian Wright

India's vast rail network traverses every terrain from the southernmost tip of the peninsula to the Himalaya. Of all these railways some have captured people's imagination more than any others. These are India's hill railways.

The oldest, the Darjeeling Himalayan Railway, or DHR, climbs through the foothills of the Eastern Himalaya, a region of high rainfall, where torrents rage during the monsoon and hillsides are clad in tree ferns and lush greenery. Over a thousand kilometres away, the Kalka-Shimla Railway snakes through the foothills of the Western Himalaya, through dryer pine covered slopes to the deodar cedar-shaded hill station of Shimla, once the summer capital of the British Raj, and now the capital of the Indian state of Himachal Pradesh. In the same state the Kangra Valley line, offers views along its length of the spectacular snow-capped Dhauladhar Range just to its north. This railway connects towns and popular pilgrimage places on the route from Pathankot to Jogindernagar. In the south, the hill station of Udagamandalam, formerly known as Ootacamund or Ooty, stands in the Nilgiris or Blue Mountains, the loftiest of the mountain ranges of this region, and here, too, a unique hill railway makes a particularly steep ascent using a rack and pinion system. ' In fact, Ooty is the only meter gauge track' which is not quite correct English. This is the sole meter gauge hill railway, as all the others run on narrow gauge. Close to Mumbai, Matheran in the Western Ghats or Sahyadaris, is the only hill station to have kept the motorcar from running through its centre. That privilege remains the preserve of the Matheran Light Railway.

Of these five, the DHR, Nilgiris and Shimla railways have been recognized jointly by UNESCO as sites of not just national, but universal importance, while, to use railway parlance, the Kangra and Matheran railways are still on the waiting list.

In 1999, the DHR was first of these railways to be given World Heritage status. The UNESCO inscription described it as 'the first, and still the most outstanding, example of a hill passenger railway…it applied bold and ingenious engineering solutions to the problem of establishing an effective rail link across a mountainous terrain of great beauty. It is still fully operational and retains most of its original features intact.'

Most impressive of these engineering solutions are the loops and Z-shaped reverses. These allow the splendid, rotund, blue, fourteen-ton B-Class steam locomotives to run on a two-foot gauge from New Jalpaiguri in the plains, 146 metres above sea level, up to Ghoom, the highest railway station in India at 2,258 metres, and then gently down to Darjeeling (2,134 metres). The railway was completed in 1881 in just eighteen months, a tribute to the skills of the men who built it and the sense of urgency with which they worked.

Like the other heritage hill railways, the DHR was constructed during the days of the British Raj. To hold India, the British needed to maintain an army and it needed its troops, particularly its British troops, to be healthy. As the borders of empire widened and the foothills of the Himalaya came under British control, the idea of sanatoria in the hills gained ground. It was believed that in the hills troops quickly recovered their health. Where the army went, civilians could not be far behind. They too craved a climate more like that of their home country. As Emily Eden, the sister of the Governor-General Lord Eden, put it during a summer in Simla, as Shimla was then known, 'Like meat, we keep better here'. The hills offered other opportunities for the Raj too, especially, as the East India Company sought a source for tea other than China.

In 1841, just two years after the first commercial tea company was founded in Assam, Dr Campbell, the Superintendent of the nascent hill station of Darjeeling, began experimenting with tea there. The bushes did well—exceptionally well in fact and, by luck rather than judgement, it was discovered that the hillsides of Darjeeling produced the world's finest high grown teas. With the establishment of the tea industry, the population grew. In 1835, the whole of Darjeeling and the land around it, granted to the British by the ruler of Sikkim, had a population of around a hundred. By 1891 that had grown to a quarter of a million, 88,000 of them born in Nepal and most of these employed on the tea estates. By 1900, there were 148 gardens in Darjeeling and over 50,000 acres under tea. The tea growers demanded a railway to transport both, themselves and their product.

Until the railway was built, troops and civilians had to make a lengthy journey from Calcutta to Siliguri at the foot of the mountains, and from there, make an uncomfortable ascent to their destination by bullock cart. Matters improved once the East Bengal Railway's line to Siliguri opened in 1878, but the final climb to Darjeeling was still a problem. Franklin Prestage, the Railway's Agent, had the idea of building a railway along the existing cart road, rather than building a separate route. He believed that this 'steam tramway', as it was originally called, would not only make Darjeeling accessible but cut down the excessive costs of cartage that more than doubled the cost of basic necessities in the hills. After one false start, on 8 April 1879 an agreement was signed between the Indian government and the Darjeeling Steam Tramway Co. with Prestage as its chairman and capital raised within India.

The British contractors relied on Indian sub-contractors and labour, skilled and unskilled, to complete the work. Terry Martin, in his book on the DHR, *Halfway to Heaven*, lists the classes and castes of workers required as 'bridge builders, carpenters, stone-cutters and bricklayers...iron-smiths, hammer-men, lifters of heavy weights, bellows boys, water carriers, storekeepers, timekeepers, interpreters, platelayers, trumpeters for mobilising people, quarrymen, brick-moulders, riveters and bullock cart drivers'. The agreement was that the railway was to be completed within two years, and so work began simultaneously along the line with the most difficult and labour intensive sections tackled among the first.

The aim was to run the railway along the 25-foot wide Hill Cart Road, which in theory was at a gradient of 1:30 with a maximum gradient of 1:25. (In ordinary terms, a slope that has a rise of 4 feet for every 100 feet of run would have a gradient of 1:25.) Later, however, it became evident that in many places—almost fifteen miles of the total length of 49 miles—the gradient was as steep as 1:20. This presented immense challenges, but the budget and time restrictions meant that there was now no scope for finding a different route. The construction of tunnels, for example, would send the project wildly over budget.

From Siliguri to the first station, Sukna, the gradient was easy to deal with, but beyond Sukna were the thick jungles of the terai—literally the 'damp area'—then teeming with wildlife including leopards, tigers and elephant. The gradient also rose, and from here the contractors' problems began in earnest and increased further up in the foothills.

One way to achieve the climb was to construct the line's famous loops, using the natural contours of the hill for the line to ascend and cross itself, forming graceful approximations to the letter 'O'. Two of the original loops have now been replaced, the first when the track was realigned and the other by a Z-shaped reverse. The three remaining are still spectacular to travel on, especially the magnificent Batasia double loop created in 1919 between Ghoom and Darjeeling. This encloses a war memorial and a riot of orange flowers, and only fresh air stands between it and the snowy mass of Mount Kanchanjunga which, together with tea and the train itself, symbolize modern Darjeeling. The two other loops are the aptly named Agony Point and the Chunbatti Loop, which circles twice around the Chunbatti Spur.

There is a well-known story, perhaps apocryphal, about the creation of the other engineering triumph, the Z-shaped 'reverse stations'. The contractor Herbert Ramsay is said to have reached a point—at the Tindharia Spur—the site of the DHR workshop—where no loop could bridge the gradient. Ramsay was at his wit's end, when his wife, remembering her lessons of ballroom dancing, remarked, 'If you're in a tight corner on the dance floor, it's perfectly all right to reverse. Why don't you just go backwards?' Inspired by this, or perhaps hearing of a technique already used once in the Western Ghats near Bombay, this is precisely what Ramsay did. The train runs forward to the edge of the slope then reverses back up the hillside where the points are changed and it runs forward and upwards, in the shape of the letter Z. The DHR has six Z reverses on its length.

Even though the opening was marred when carriages, full of officials, jumped the track and had to be levered back, the line was popular from the start. It changed its name from a tramway to a railway, and was managed by Gillanders Arbuthnot & Co., one of the leading management agencies of Calcutta. It was still running profitably when in October 1948, just over a year after independence, it was purchased by the Indian government. Currently, it forms part of the North-East Frontier Railway with its headquarters at Guwahati. The line has been extended to New Jalpaiguri in the plains, and diesel locomotives have been introduced.

There are fourteen stations, most of them designed like English cottages. They include the original southern terminus of Siliguri, the picturesque gables of Sukna, Kurseong, Tindharia with its locomotive works and skilled engineers, and Ghoom, which, as well as being the highest station, is also one of the biggest and often is the place to find the working heritage locomotives all steamed up. The journey from the city, through the terai forests and then the tea estates to Darjeeling, is a total of 88 kilometres.

The instability of the hillsides during the monsoon has, however, always endangered this unique heritage asset. In 2010, a major landslide breached the track and the road at Pagla Jhora—literally 'the mad stream'—and the next two monsoons saw major landslips at Tindharia. These landslides effectively divided the route—with steam and diesel services between Kurseong and Darjeeling on the upper part, and a diesel-hauled rail safari between Siliguri and Chunbatti on the lower. Throughout these difficulties, the Indian Railways have shown their determination to keep the DHR open.

While diesel has its advantages, it is the steam engines that are the star attraction. These indestructible 0-4-0 tank engines, to quote the late railway historian and engineer Michael Satow, 'exemplify the basic, simple steam locomotive at its best'. As he put it, 'their design has remained unsurpassed'. The oldest of the thirteen original locomotives still in regular use was built in 1889. It has left India, and now hauls trains on heritage lines in England. The remaining twelve are still to be found on the DHR and four of these, manufactured in 1893, 1898, 1904 and 1913, have completed their centuries. While the first two were built at the Atlas Works in Glasgow, the majority of the others were made at the North British Locomotive Company in the same city. However, one came from Philadelphia in the United States in 1917 and one was constructed at the railway's own Tindharia workshop in 1919. There is a fourteenth working locomotive too, but it's a youngster. Converted from oil to coal, it was built in south India in 2003.

These wonderful examples of engineering require constant loving care. Each steam-hauled, manually-braked passenger train has a crew of seven. Apart from the driver there are two firemen to look after the locomotive's firebox, boiler and maintenance, and three brakesman whose duties include applying hand brakes on the downhill stretches and sanding the track on the uphill gradient to improve the wheels' grip. The last member of the crew is a Guard Jamadar who monitors the train's operation at all the reverse points, controls the train at road level crossings and helps in shunting. Their teamwork is worth seeing, and undoubtedly one of the reasons why steam charters and joyrides on the DHR prove so popular.

Where Darjeeling led, could Simla be far behind? Officially declared the summer capital of the British Raj in 1864, every year the viceroy and his government travelled across the plains from Calcutta, and up into the Shivalik Hills to this ridge over 2,200 metres above sea level, overlooking the snowy peaks of the

Himalaya. This immense journey was made immeasurably easier as the railways advanced, and in March 1891 the line finally reached Kalka, at the foot of the hills.

The earliest survey for a railway from Kalka to Simla was made in 1884. However, the steepness of the ascent made it clear that on this route, a railway running alongside the road, would not work. There was intense and prolonged debate on what else to try. A rope incline was suggested, where the train would be hauled up steep sections by ropes, and also a rack and pinion system, where a gear wheel under the train fits into notched rails under the train, allowing it to negotiate steeper inclines than the conventional adhesion system used across the plains. This was proposed as a cheaper option, but finally the adhesion system won, with the gauge at two feet and a gradient no steeper than 1:33. The Delhi-Ambala-Kalka Railway Company, that signed a contract with the government to build the railway in 1898, was given harsh terms for such a capital-intensive project—no government guarantees or aid—although land was given free. But the company had to accommodate another major change. Under a new policy, railways, for strategic purposes, should have a standard gauge of two-feet-six-inches. The company had no choice but to widen the gauge accordingly.

The line therefore, although inspired by the DHR, was vastly different in conception. Not only did it have a wider gauge, while the DHR avoided tunnels, the Kalka-Simla railway relied upon them—originally 107 of them along its 96-kilometers length, of which 103 are still in use. Due to the unstable nature of the hills, these presented great challenges to the engineers. One of the most difficult tunnels to construct was No. 2, on the line near Dharampur. Passing through clay and shale, the walls bulged dangerously. Only by shoring them up with heavy timber was it possible to avoid a total collapse and it took a further eight months before the tunnel was completed.

The longest tunnel, No. 33 and 3,752 feet (1,144 metres) long, is at Barog. As pointed out by G.S. Khosla in his *A History of the Indian Railways*, the tunnel has one long welded rail, a kilometre in length, the only one of its kind on the narrow gauge in India. The picturesque cottage-style station, 900 feet below the main road, is a haven of peace, bedecked with hanging baskets of flowers and pots of geraniums. This was and remains the natural place to have breakfast on the route up. Sausages and bacon have long since disappeared from the menu, but piping hot cutlets, omelettes and tea are much in demand. Visitors mull over the tragic story of Colonel Barog, after whom the station is named. The engineer in charge of constructing the tunnel, he committed suicide after the two ends of the tunnel failed to meet.

Another unique characteristic of this railway is that ravines along the route are bridged by handsome multi-tiered stone arches resembling the aqueducts of ancient Rome. Particularly fine examples can be seen near Dharampur where the line makes a beautiful S bend up the mountainside. The railway has at total of 869 bridges as it ascends the mountains in a series of reverse curves.

Opened in 1903, such had been the enormous investment involved that the Company was deep in debt. Not only was the line expensive to build, it was, and is still, expensive to maintain, especially due to monsoon landslides and winter snow. It has been recorded that in 1904 the company had invested ₹16,525,000 in the project and found the only sensible way ahead was to sell the KSR to the government. As the line was invaluable for the British, the government agreed and purchased the railway in January 1906.

Shimla is now the permanent home of the state government of Himachal Pradesh and attracts thousands of visitors, many of whom still consider the train journey an essential part of their holiday experience. Regular services run throughout the year, but even more run in summer, to meet the rush of people escaping the heat of the plains. In my experience, there is nothing like the joy of travelling up to Shimla in the single-coach railcar, which allows incredible views of the track ahead, or the pleasure of looking out of the train windows in the monsoon when, at sunset, rosy clouds settle in green valleys below. The journey takes between four hours forty-five minutes and five hours twenty minutes, depending on how many of the line's 22 stations the train stops at.

Not all passengers travel all the way to Shimla as the line links many other important hill towns. Heading up from Kalka (653 metres), passengers for Kasauli, a charming hill station and cantonment on the first high ridge of the Shivaliks, get down at Dharampur (1,469 metres). The now large and sprawling town of Solan (1,494 metres) is another major stop. Its brewery, moved from its original position at Kasauli, is the oldest in Asia and has a station all of its own. The line then descends to Kandaghat station (1,432 metres), the closest point to Chail the summer seat of the Maharaja of Patiala, and site of perhaps the highest cricket pitch in the world. From Kandaghat the final climb to Shimla begins. Summer Hill (2,043 metres), only a short distance from Shimla station (2,075 metres), is famous as the Viceroy's station as he could step down from his regal carriage here and climb to the baronial Viceroy's Lodge on the ridge above. But the highest point on the line is New Shimla station, originally an extension for loading goods—principally the region's famous winter potatoes—and now the site of the railway's museum, at 2,094 metres. Although steam has long since been replaced by diesel, one of the original locomotives has been renovated and should become available for special chartered runs

While the officials of the Raj were trying to decide how to build a railway to their summer capital, another very distinct railway, the Nilgiri Mountain Railway, was already under construction. This is the only metre-gauge hill railway in India, and the only one to use the rack and pinion system that, we have seen, was ultimately rejected for the Simla railway.

The British took control of Nilgiris, or Blue Mountains, the home of the pastoral Toda tribal community, after they defeated Tipu Sultan, the ruler of Mysore, in 1799. The hills were incorporated into the Madras Presidency in 1818, after which two young assistants of the Collector of Coimbatore went on an expedition into the mountains and 'discovered' a plateau of green pastureland and patches of forest that was later developed as the hill station of Ootacamund or Ooty, now called Udagamandalam. The Nilgiris provided an almost English climate—with the notable exception of the monsoon—and attracted both the armed forces and civilians, from British officials to Indian princes. Below Ooty sprang up the hill station of Coonoor. Tea was planted and today, Nilgiri high-grown teas are considered to be of extremely fine quality.

In 1891, the first sod of the hill railway to Ooty was cut by Lord Wenlock, the Governor of Madras (now Chennai). The original railway company ran into financial trouble and was taken over by another, and so it wasn't until 1899 that the stretch from Mettupalayam in the plains to Coonoor was fully operable. In 1903, the government took over the line and under the supervision of the engineers, C.F. Sykes and H. Gales, the 12-mile section from Coonoor to Ooty was finally completed five years later. At Coonoor, trains must reverse a short distance before continuing

> At Coonoor, trains must reverse a short distance before continuing their climb to Ooty.

their climb to Ooty.

For the traveller, although the whole of the 46-kilometres line is beautiful, nothing competes with the excitement of a journey in the early morning on the 28-kilometres stretch between Mettupalayam, site of the main steam engine shed, and Coonoor (1,712 metres). The mountains appear as blue as their name as the early morning train sets off along a normal adhesion track over the Bhavani river to Kallar (405 metres). Here the rack and pinion section begins, as the train leaves the station the gradient is an amazing 1:12, steeper than any other heritage mountain railway in Asia. In this section alone, there are 208 curves, 13 tunnels and 27 viaducts.

Six of the superb original blue-liveried 0-8-2 X-Class steam engines designed and built in the Swiss Locomotive Works in Winerthur, Switzerland, still propel passengers upwards through the thick forest of this section. Two of these date from as far back as 1918, while the other four date from 1949 and 1950. As diesel locomotives cannot be adapted to the rack and pinion system, the old locos share their duties with three new oil-fired steam locomotives, manufactured specially at Southern Railway's Golden Rock Workshop in Tiruchirappalli between 2011 and 2013. These weigh 50 tonnes, can pull 97.6 tonnes, and can reach a speed of 30 kilometres per hour in the plains and 15 kilometres per hour on a gradient.

The train chugs up past Adderly, a water stop, before pausing at Hillgrove Station, 18 kilometres up the line, where bonnet macaque, with their blue eyelids and neat centre partings, are very happy to help to finish off the fresh breakfast of steaming hot idlis, vadas and sweet bananas available from the light refreshment stall on the platform. Monkeys are not the only wildlife on the line. This is elephant country. Every day, before the morning train departs, railway employees inspect the line on foot, and the return train leaves sufficiently early to reduce the risk of meeting wild elephants. From Hillgrove the train toils through rough-hewn, smoke-blackened tunnels up to the first tea gardens. Passing through Runneymede and Kateri Road stations, it steams into the town of Coonoor. Here the steepest part of the journey is over and the rack and pinion section comes to an end. The exhausted engine is uncoupled and replaced by a diesel locomotive.

Beyond Coonoor, the track levels out and the landscape is more tame. The next stop is elegant Wellington (1,769.1 metres), a cantonment town famous for the prestigious Defence Services Staff College, a training institution for officers of the armed forces, that is situated here. The line then passes through to Arunvankadu, Ketti and Lovedale, the highest station at 2,345 metres before reaching the end of the line, Udhagamandalam Station, at 7,228 feet/2,203 metres with all its modernity, its thousands of visitors, and its heritage buildings. This memorable journey takes nearly five hours on the way up and just over three and a half on the way down.

Like Ooty, Matheran in the Western Ghats, presents a very different landscape to the Himalayan foothills. Unlike Ooty, it's virtually on the doorstep of an Indian metropolis, being a mere 90 kilometres east of Mumbai, earlier known as Bombay. The collector of Thane, Hugh Poyntz Malet, was the first British official to be impressed by Matheran's natural beauty—its dark green jambol forests and viewpoints around the plateau's edge overlooking the plains—when he visited in 1850. Subsequently, the Governor of Bombay, Lord Elphinstone, popularized Matheran by staying there himself. It soon became the favourite holiday destination of Indians from Bombay as well, particularly, the prosperous Bohra Muslim and Parsi families.

Matheran was and remains unique among India's hill stations. Firstly, it is the only one to prohibit motor transport—cars and buses are stopped 3 kilometres from the centre of the town. Secondly, its railway is the only one entirely financed and built by Indians. The entrepreneur, Sir Adamjee Peerbhoy of Bombay, personally financed the project that was the brainchild of his son Abdul Hussein. Abdul Hussein played a leading role in the development of Matheran as a whole, and put his heart and soul into his dream railway. Four years went into the planning. Work started in 1904, the gauge being 2 feet, the same as the DHR. Abdul Hussein brought his wife and children from Bombay to Neral, the starting point of the new line, to be near the construction. And, with his engineer, also an Indian, known as Rao Sahib, he journeyed into the forests supervising the work and in the process confronting large numbers of poisonous snakes. When the railway was complete he rode on the footplate of the first locomotive to make the entire trip. Well-wishers cautioned him against risking his safety, but he was quick to reply that the engine driver and crew's lives were just as precious as his own. In the event the journey went exactly as planned. The line was opened for the public in 1907 and proved a most profitable enterprise.

Twenty kilometres long, the railway climbs from Neral, site of the locomotive shed and workshops, through 221 curves and a tunnel so short that it is known as the 'One Kiss Tunnel', to Matheran station at 809 metres, the journey taking around two hours. The gradient reaches 1:20 generally on the curves, where a clever engineering technique known as 'compensation' slightly lessens the gradient. The principal steam engines used on the line were 0-6-0 T locomotives with a special flexible wheelbase, known

> Matheran railway is the only one entirely financed and built by Indians.

A view of a bridge.

A half-tunnel on Nilgiri Mountain Railway.

Bridge in the Pathankot–Jogindernagar section of the Kangra Valley Railway

Palampur railway station (it was within the state of Punjab).

Palampur railway station (after the new state of Himachal Pradesh was carved out of Punjab).

An old photograph of a rail car on Neral–Matheran section.

A waterfall on the Neral–Matheran section.

Different sections on the Matheran Light Railway.

An old photograph of a train on the Darjeeling Himalayan Railway.

The picturesque Batasia Loop on the Darjeeling Himalayan Railway.

Ghum railway station on the Darjeeling Himalayan Railway.

An old photograph of a train arriving at the Barog station on the Kalka-Shimla railway.

A recent photograph of the Barog tunnel on the Kalka–Shimla railway.

A rail car on the Kalka-Shimla railway

The Kannoh Bridge on the Kalka-Shimla railway.

poetically as floating axles, to cope with the sharp bends and climbs. Although the locos have retired, they have all been preserved and one of them—MLR loco No. 741 made in 1905—is on permanent display at Matheran railway station. Apart from steam, the line also operated railcars that were converted road transport buses with petrol engines. After independence, the track was upgraded and diesel locomotives have been used since 1955, with the occasional steam special.

The Western Ghats bear the initial brunt of the onslaught of the Southwest monsoon, and for many years the Matheran line was shut during these months. This is now no longer necessarily, although falling boulders and landslides do interrupt services. I have myself witnessed how swiftly maintenance teams are on site, moving huge boulders with crowbars. Barring monsoon closures, visitors continue to enjoy the journey from the Neral, up to Jummapatti and Bekra Khud, under the shadow of Mount Barry, through 'One Kiss Tunnel' to a station called 'Water Pipe', where steam engines would once take on water. Passengers now take tea here, before the train leaves for Aman Lodge where the road ends. Central Railway, now responsible for the MLR, recently responded to public demand by starting a shuttle service between Aman Lodge and Matheran. The shuttle runs even at the height of the monsoon. Not only is this immensely popular with tourists, it provides a solution to the longstanding problem of transporting supplies from the roadhead to the town. Beyond Aman Lodge, the line embraces Panorama Point before reaching Matheran whose glorious surrounding landscape is now protected as an eco-sensitive region.

The youngest of India's hill railways is perhaps the longest operating heritage railway in the world. Stretching over 163 kilometres, instead of climbing from the plains towards the summit of the hills, like India's other heritage hill railways, it traverses the length of the rural, verdant Kangra Valley at the foot of the 2,500-5,000 metres Dhauladhar Range of the Himalaya. The valley rises in altitude as it runs from west to east. Until the Kangra Valley railway was built this valley was accessible only on foot or by animal transport, and so it has served as a cultural corridor linking towns, holiday destinations like picturesque Palampur, and pilgrimage places. However, it was created for a different purpose—to carry men and equipment as close as possible to the Uhl River Hydro Electric Works that were opened in 1929 to provide electricity to Punjab.

Work on the line between Pathankot, the railhead and major Punjab town, and the terminus at Jogindernagar began in 1926 and the railway was opened for freight at the end of 1928 and for passenger traffic three months later on 1 April 1929. Although the line lacks the steep gradients of other hill railways, it still presented the engineers with enormous challenges as here, too, they had to contend with mountainous territory and raging torrents. Gradients reach 1:25, and they had to construct 993 bridges, 2 tunnels and 484 curves.

Just over a decade after the line was opened, it was considered uneconomic and therefore dispensible enough for over fifty kilometres of track between Nagrota and Jogindernagar to be dismantled and dispatched in order to be used by the Allies in the Second World War. The line was only rebuilt after Independence, when it was inaugurated by the Railway Minister and future Prime Minister, Lal Bahadur Shastri, in 1954. In 1973, about 25 kilometres of the track had to be realigned due to the creation of the Pong Dam. Two major bridges were constructed on this portion of the line—the Dehar Bridge and the New Gaj Bridge.

Despite these changes, the railway retains its heritage character. The signalling system, linked to the carrying of spherical metal tokens from one station to the next, dates from 1926. Most of the girder bridges and the half-timbered stations, with their pitched roofs and deep verandahs are very much as they always were, and although steam is no longer used on the line one 2-6-2-ZB-Class locomotive, manufactured in Britain in 1952, has been restored for special chartered trains.

Like other hill railways this one too has suffered the vagaries of the monsoon. The Chakki Bridge, just twelve kilometres from Pathankot on the lowest section of the line, has been repeatedly damaged by flash floods in the rivulet below, apparently exacerbated by mining of the riverbed for sand and stones. This is one of the first remarkable bridges of the railway, which on this initial section has a gentle maximum gradient of 1:40.

From the Chakki Bridge, the line becomes steeper. This 130-kilometre section runs to the Hindu pilgrimage centre of Baijnath Patprola (980 metres) and nearby Baijnath Mandir Halt, site of a Shiva temple dating to the ninth century and enshrining one of India's 12 jyotirlinga, symbolizing Shiva as a column of light. On the way the line passes through Nurpur Road, the town being named after the Mughal Emperor Jahangir's queen Nur Jahan, who is said to have fallen in love with its beauty. The town's ruined fort and temples are its major attraction for visitors. Between Jawali and Nagrota Suriyan, the line curves around the hills and skirts the scenic Pong reservoir, before heading to Guler. The Indian rulers of the Kangra Valley established not only forts, palaces and temples but were great patrons of art and in particular miniature painting, with very distinct delicate and graceful styles. Guler was one

The author, Ruskin Bond, has written about the KVR that it is 'proof that the railway engineer can create a work which is in complete harmony with the beauty of the surroundings'.

such centre. Beyond the line crosses the dramatic Banganga Gorge and reaches Jwalamukhi Road, the station for the famous temple to the goddess Jawalamukhi, literally flame-mouthed, built over flames of natural gas, 20 kilometres away.

The line then turns to the north, crossing another remarkable bridge before entering the line's two tunnels, 79-metres and 327-metres long, and reaching Kangra, the former capital of the Chand rajas. The views of the snows between Kangra and Palampur are spectacular, and Palampur, with its heritage railway bungalow, still has a peaceful, old-fashioned charm with its Mall, heritage hotel, and tea estates.

The final 22 kilometres of the line runs at a gradient of 1:25 through the pine-clad slopes of the Bir Gorge, away from the road. The highest station on the railway, Ajhu (1,210 metres), is on this section. Particularly attractive, it is close to a flourishing Tibetan centre. Jogindernagar (1,184 metres) is the last of the 31 stations and halts on the line. The entire journey on one of the faster trains from Pathankot takes six hours forty-five minutes.

The author, Ruskin Bond, has written about the KVR, that it is 'proof that the railway engineer can create a work which is in complete harmony with the beauty of the surroundings'. These are words of praise that can be applied to every one of India's distinct narrow gauge hill railways. Each has a different character, but each complements the surrounding landscape besides providing an enjoyable and eco-friendly way to travel through the hills. Loved by visitors and by residents alike, it goes very much to the credit of Indian Railways and their dedicated staff, that to this day these railways, all of them treasures of railway heritage, are maintained and kept alive.

THE LIFELINE OF THE NATION

Sharmila Kantha

Railway Operations

The Indian Railways (IR) is rightly described as 'the lifeline of the nation'. The fourth largest railway network and freight carrier in the world and the second largest for passenger traffic, it is of critical importance to India's economic development in its various roles as transport facility, service provider and manufacturer. It would not be an exaggeration to say that the Indian Railways reaches out to each and every citizen in various ways.

With over 64,000 kilometres of route length, the Indian Railways is also the world's second largest rail network under a single management system. If one were to count total trackage, including yards, sidings, etc., and stretch out the rails in a single line, that line would go around the Equator almost three times, or reach one-third of the way to the moon.[4]

---

[4]Taking length of the Equator at 40,000 kilometres, distance to moon at 384,000 kilometres and tracks at 114,000 kilometres

Even though the Indian Railways is omnipresent, its operational aspect is not common knowledge. The railways have the responsibility of not only planning new routes and building new lines, but also to upgrade and maintain existing tracks, look after more than 7,000 stations, and undertake all related activities for smooth operation. These include setting up and maintaining the entire signals network, carrying out electrification and single gauge projects, manufacturing wagons and carriages, and looking after its staff. Consider this statistic: the total track kilometres—which was around 78,000 kilometres in 1950-51—has increased to 115,000 kilometres in 2011-12. It's quite staggering.

Another activity that has continued—efficiently and rapidly—is the electrification of rail tracks. The painstaking efforts of the railways have led to almost 20,000 route kilometres being electrified. The Eleventh Five Year Plan (2007-08 to 2011-12) in particular set high targets for electrification and more than 4,500 kilometres of route was completed. The list of impressive statistics is furthered by the fact that between 1950-51 and 2011-12, traffic density calculated in million gross tonne kilometres per running track kilometre increased from 4.29 to 23.17 on broad-gauge.[5]

One more proud achievement is the fact that almost all production for the railways is undertaken indigenously, mostly through manufacturing centres owned and operated by the Indian Railways, with a small proportion coming from private producers. In 2011-12, the Indian Railways had some 9,500 engines and almost 230,000 wagons. Axles and wheels, spare parts, passenger coach amenities, signals, and in fact, the entire range of ancillary items required by trains are produced in-house with less than 10 per cent of the total stores imported. The factories are spread over the

---

[5]http://indianrailways.gov.in/railwayboard/uploads/directorate/stat_econ/yearbook11-12/Track_bridges.pdf

country, providing employment to thousands of workers directly and supporting communities indirectly. This is no small feat given that *everything* was once imported.

Notably, between 1950-51 and 2011-12, the growth in freight carried by the Indian Railways has been over ten times, while passenger traffic has multiplied by seven.[6] All this was achieved during a time when the number of engines barely went up (from 8,200 to 9,500) and the number of wagons in operation hardly increased.[7]

This shows how far the railways have expanded productivity. Despite constraints, the Indian Railways has survived through local innovations, setting strong systems in place to match resources to requirements.

The services provided by the Indian Railways extend over multiple areas. The most important of these are carrying freight and movement of passengers, both of which are, in fact, done over the same tracks and therefore require much coordination and planning. The railways carried over one billion tonnes of freight during 2012-13[8], double the volume of 2000-01, representing about a third of total movement of goods in the country. A wide variety of commodities including bulk cargo such as coal, iron ore, fertilizers, cement, steel, etc. as well as

> Despite constraints, the Indian Railways has survived through local innovations, setting strong systems in place to match resources to requirements.

---

[6]Economic Survey 2012-13
[7]Second Plan document http://planningcommission.nic.in/plans/planrel/fiveyr/index1.html
[8]PIB http://www.pib.nic.in/newsite/erelease.aspx?relid=94606

specialized goods such as vehicles are transported across the country over rail. In 2011-12, 8.2 billion passenger journeys were tallied by train[9], which is one fifth of all passenger traffic[10], with a total distance of 10 lakh kilometres being travelled.[11] Every day, the Indian Railways carries the equivalent of Australia's entire population on its trains.

All these activities are carried out by just over 14 lakh workers employed currently, which also makes the Indian Railways among the biggest civilian employers in the world. It is even more interesting to note that in 1950-51, it employed as many as 9.13 lakh workers. The enormity of these achievements gets magnified further when you think of how this tremendous increase in volume is managed with just five lakh more employees. The railways have accomplished this by dramatically increasing worker productivity. Seven Centralized Training Institutes hone the talents of railway officers, and another 270 training centres across the country meet the learning needs of the non-gazetted staff. At the same time, expenditure on staff has gone up eleven times in this period.[12] Despite government mandated wages and salary structures, the Indian Railways has been able to meet staff expenses from its own resources. Industrial relations in the railways are stronger than anywhere else in the country and the trade unions are considered an important advantage for the Indian Railways. There have been no labour strikes since 1974—as compared to the corporate sector or other public sector undertakings where labour unrest is frequent.

Apart from these core functions, the railways also provide

---

[9]Economic Survey 2012-13
[10]*Rail Transportation in India: Moving to the Next Orbit*, CII background paper for International Rail Conference, 28 September 2011
[11]Year Book 2011-12
[12]Year Book 2011-12

related services to businesses and passengers, such as hotels and restaurants, food on board the trains, maintenance and upkeep of stations, and other functions, which can be described as non-core. Additionally, a new avenue of activity has opened up in the form of consultancy and construction services overseas through its subsidiary organizations. For example, Ircon International Limited (IRCON) has built over 90 projects in 21 countries, many of them under difficult conditions.[13]

What Ails the Indian Railways?

Despite its successes, it is to be noted that the Indian Railways has much to achieve in terms of performance, modernization and technology absorption and is significantly overstretched in meeting the expectations of a rapidly growing modern economy. This has become increasingly difficult given the social responsibility that is expected of the railways. The Indian Railways spends hundreds of crores in maintaining 125 hospitals with 14,000 hospital beds and over 2,500 doctors and 54,000 paramedical staff to look after lakhs of current and former employees. No other successful railway in the world needs to allocate funds towards this.

While the social responsibility of the Indian Railways is undeniably critical to the vision of inclusive growth within India,

---

[13]IRCON website

there are times when some of the projects, which are undertaken to increase regional connectivity purely on socio-economic considerations, are not financially viable. These large investments are made to serve the backward and less developed regions without any expectation of financial returns.

So, What Exactly Is the Situation?

According to the Twelfth Plan (2012-13 to 2016-17) paper, the average speed of freight trains in India is 25 kilometres per hour, about half the speed of that in the US. The share of rail in transporting goods at about one-third compares poorly to the 48 per cent in the US and the 47 per cent in China[14], while India transports just about a fourth of the freight per kilometre carried by China.[15] The Working Group Report for the Twelfth Plan notes that network productivity of Chinese railways is more than double that of the Indian Railways, while employee productivity is higher by half. The Indian economy is dependent on the Indian Railways' ecosystem in different ways, and a lack of healthy infrastructure and operations constrains overall productivity. For one, the competitiveness of industry does not live up to its full potential. Key industry sectors such as steel, mining, ports, etc. depend on the Indian Railways for their regular operations. The demand is for stability, speed, and efficiency in the transport of raw materials and finished goods and customers are willing to pay in return for quality services.

Due to inadequate resources, the Indian Railways route network has expanded by barely 1,600 kilometres over the last

---

[14]Twelfth Five Year Plan, Economic Sectors, page 196
[15]Dhara, Tushar and Krishnan, Unni, 'Walking Pace Trains Spur $17 billion India Rail Revamp', 15 Feb 2013, *Bloomberg*, bloomberg.com

decade. In this time, China has created an entirely new high-speed rail network of 10,000 kilometres, opening up new economic opportunities for a hundred connected cities and taking its route length to over 100,000 kilometres.

When it comes to aligning the Indian Railways with the requirements of a modern industrial economy, it falls short in terms of planning, investment, technology adoption, safety and other parameters. Over the Eleventh Plan, Indian Railways suffered cumulative losses in passenger services of almost ₹80,000 crores, despite the improvement in the first three years. Between 2007-08 and 2008-09, the loss doubled to ₹14,000 crores[16], and was expected to touch ₹25,000 crores in 2013-14.[17] Thus, in over just a decade, the accumulated losses of the Indian Railways from passenger services could be more than ₹1,50,000 crores.

This is compounded by a skewed tariff system where passenger fares are cross-subsidized from freight rates. This leaves no room for expansion and modernization of passenger services as also discourages movement of freight by rail. While passenger fares are one-fourth of China's, and just one-twentieth of Japan's, the Indian Railways' freight rates are among the highest in the world[18]. According to the Twelfth Plan document, freight rates in China, Russia and the US are as low as 58 per cent, 75 per cent and 51 per cent respectively of freight rates in India. These figures are clearly unsustainable and impede the Indian Railways' role as an instrument of economic growth.

There are several reasons for the sub-par performance of the Indian Railways. For one, dwindling government support is a major cause for low capital investment in the Indian Railways.

---

[16]Twelfth Plan Economic Sectors
[17]Railway Budget 2013-14 Speech of Railway Minister Pawan Kumar Bansal
[18]Twelfth Plan Economic Sectors pp 213

For example, in the Second Plan, total outlay proposed for railway development was ₹900 crores, of which ₹150 crores was to be generated internally. By the Eleventh Plan, of the total investment of ₹1.92 lakh crore, only ₹77,039 crores came from government support, while ₹66,000 crores were generated internally and ₹44,000 crores from extra-budgetary resources like market borrowings. This expenditure fell short of planned outlay during the five years by over ₹40,000 crores[19].

In terms of government support to railways as a proportion of the GDP, India thus comes in poorly at 0.25 per cent.[20] For example, the UK spent an average of 0.35 per cent of its GDP on rail infrastructure investment alone during 1995-2008, while Germany registers 0.27 per cent, in addition to subsidy expenses and rolling stock investments.[21] When we consider that the GDP of these countries is far higher than that of India, while the length of their tracks is far smaller, it is obvious that per kilometre of track, public investment in railways in the country is much below the required expenditure levels.

Apart from lack of adequate central government support, there is barely any role or funding by state governments, which are major beneficiaries of railway systems in their jurisdiction. In recent

---

[19]Twelfth Plan document

[20]₹21,000 crores as per Revised Budget estimates for 2011-12 (Twelfth Plan document) as percentage of the GDP at factor cost at current prices ₹83,53,495 crores (Economic Survey 2012-13)

[21]'A Fare Return: Ensuring the UK's railways deliver true value for money' Just Economics https://www.google.co.kr/url?sa=t&rct=j&q=&esrc=s&sour ce=web&cd=1&ved=0CCIQFjAA&url=http%3a%2f%2fwww%2ejustecono mics%2eco%2euk%2fapp%2fdownload%2f6341337350%2fXA_Fare_Return_ final%2epdf%3ft%3d1360515869&ei=DKX9UoW9ObCe7AbUjYCoBg&u sg=AFQjCNEtfRUOL1qRK9JekPkiIREK8S_5BQ&bvm=bv.61190604,d. aGc&cad=rjt

years, some state governments—such as Karnataka, Jharkhand, Maharashtra, Andhra Pradesh and Haryana—have come forward to invest in particular railway building projects, and such initiatives can be expanded.

A second most critical issue in railway performance is that of tariff. The Railway Board has the authority to change tariffs, but political considerations are superimposed on this. The result is that passenger tariffs have been remarkably problematic, particularly in the last decade. While the price index has doubled from 2004-05 to 2011-12, passenger ticket rates were not raised during this period. With a subsidy burden of ₹25,000 crores in 2013-14, enhanced freight rates have supplemented railway revenues and thus the Indian Railways has lost transportation share to roads.

To obviate this issue, the government decided to set up the Rail Tariff Regulatory Authority as an independent body to fix tariffs for both passengers and freight. This was expected to ameliorate the skewed balance of fares and freight rates, while also increasing productivity and performance. Most of all, it would insulate tariff levels from political interventions. There were some concerns that such an authority would be only an advisory body and moreover, would override Indian Railways' social obligations in favour of commercial considerations. However, the need to ensure long-term financial health of the railways as well as to rationalize fare-freight ratio tilted the scale towards the establishment of such an authority. It was expected that the Authority would consult with all stakeholders for a new pricing regime through a transparent process.

Third, Indian Railways also pays dividends to the central government on the gross budgetary support provided to it. During 2013-14, almost ₹5,400 crores was handed over to the central exchequer, an amount that it could ill afford. While the dividend is payable at the rate of five per cent, the return of the Indian Railways' capital investments ranges around four per cent. This makes it a tall order. This raises questions on the level of support the government is willing to provide through budgetary resources for the development of the railways.

It is equally evident that the Indian Railways bears high social responsibility. For the millions of poor passengers who travel on trains, the affordability of tickets is the main concern, along with safety. Migrants, daily commuters, pilgrims and tourists are dependent on the low-cost travel network that the Indian Railways provides. Efficiency, productivity and access to quality facilities are of little concern to them. In parts of the country where there are no rail tracks, ordinary households suffer from lack of adequate access to higher-income jobs and livelihoods. A balance has to be struck between the different roles and responsibilities of the Indian Railways, and to find this balance in order to meet divergent but imperative objectives is a challenging task.

It is clear that the approach towards the working of the Indian railway system has to be changed to encompass economic objectives. The experiences of other infrastructure sectors in India have demonstrated that a subsidy-led approach hampers expansion and access to public or semi-public goods and services. Hence, a corporate approach to restructuring of the Indian Railways may be considered for helping it attain its fullest potential as a key player in the Indian economy. The process has already started with the setting up of different undertakings such as the Dedicated Freight Corridor Corporation of India Ltd. (DFCCIL) and other public sector undertakings such as the Rail Vikas Nigam Limited (RVNL), the Rail Land Development Authority (RLDA) and the Indian Railway Catering and the Tourism Corporation (IRCTC). The challenge is to convert the Indian Railways into an effective and productive organization that will work towards lowering costs for both passenger and freight services.

Rail Systems in Other Countries

In this context, it may be useful to explore how other countries have dealt with the modernization of their railway systems. In general, modernization is a lengthy procedure, extending over several years. Historically, railways were developed by private funding and ownership with state support. After the Second World War, railway companies in many countries were nationalized. However, governments did not emerge as efficient providers of crucial rail passenger and freight services, suffering huge losses that were untenable.

Thus, from the 1990s onwards, railway systems were restructured in many countries. The main effort was to bring in corporate management, accounting and efficiency in a model that placed the government at 'arms-length' of these organizations. Primarily, the railway restructuring effort centred around three principles—distancing railways from governmental control, bringing in professional management with the objective of meeting the needs of customers, and focusing on core functions while spinning off non-core activities. Key public service responsibilities were clearly defined which were to be met from government coffers. The commercial and social services were demarcated and separated, so that business performance measures could be instituted for each.

European Union: In 1991, the EU mandated the separation of rail infrastructure and rail operators across the member nations in order to allow 'open access'. The various arms of the national rail systems were expected to run on commercial lines. The idea behind restructuring the EU rail system was to open the rail transport market to competition, improve interoperability and safety, and develop rail transport infrastructure.

According to the EU directives, 'Different organizational entities must be set up for transport operations on the one hand and infrastructure management on the other. Essential functions such as allocation of rail capacity (the "train paths" that companies need to be able to operate trains on the network), infrastructure charging and licensing must be separated from the operation of transport services and performed in a neutral fashion to give new rail operators fair access to the market. Moreover it must be guaranteed that public funds for the infrastructure and for the payment of compensation for transport services under public service obligations may not be used to finance transport operations, in order to avoid distortions of competition and an unfair use of public money.' [22]

The EU model is essentially about dividing a large organization into smaller, independent entities.

United Kingdom: The British Railways was set up in 1948 when four large private railway companies were nationalized. It became an independent statutory corporation in 1962 and routes and passenger services that were not productive were shut down. In 1982, the British Railways was divided up into three core sectors, and between 1994 and 1997, the system was privatized with a complex model of fragmentation.

---

[22] http://ec.europa.eu/transport/modes/rail/market/index_en.htm

Construction of a rail bridge.

Construction of the new bridge on the Mahanadi.

Bridge construction on the Western Freight Corridor, near Thane.

A ballast retainer wall being built.

Vallarpadam bridge on the Edapally–Vallarpadam section.

IRCTC's Maharajas' Express.

Double stack container train.

Pir Panjal tunnel in Kashmir.

Pir Panjal tunnel.

A view of Rail Neer bottling plant.

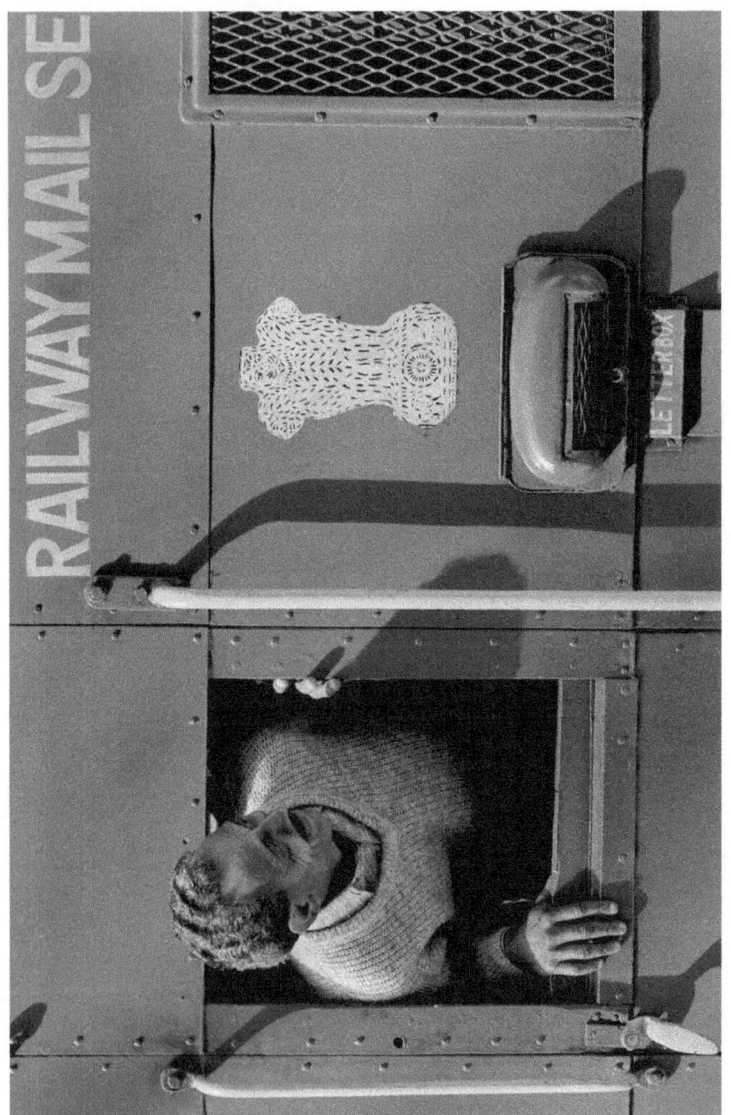

Railway mail service.

Privatization led to a separate entity, Railtrack, for track and infrastructure creation and maintenance, which was operated as a company with shareholdings and on a commercial basis but regulated by an independent regulator, the Office of Rail Regulation. Freight services were hived off completely to several private players, including from overseas, rolling stock was sold to three different companies and passenger services were franchised to twenty-five operators or Train Operating Companies, in the private sector. The operators leased rolling stock from the Rolling Stock Companies (ROSCOS) and passenger fare was regulated by another regulator, the Office of Passenger Rail Franchising.

This system did not work too well as Railtrack did not garner enough funds for growth as was expected. In 2002, it was taken over by Network Rail, a company with no shareholders and limited by guarantee. This entity raises bonds for its operations to 'run, operate, maintain and invest in Britain's rail network'. The government has returned to rail services through Directly Operated Railways—a temporary arrangement to run the East Coast line until it is refranchized—and a heated debate has arisen about bringing the railways back under the fold of the government as privatization has not lived up to expectations.

Germany: Under the EU requirements, the country has separated the infrastructure and operating companies as well as the accounts of the freight and passenger services. Deutsche Bahn (DB) is a joint-stock corporation, but owned by the government. The restructuring of the German railways was additionally necessitated by the unification of East and West Germany, where the former suffered from low technology and the latter had not invested adequately in rail routes. In 1999, DB was reformed again with nine business units through a multi-level group of companies, which separately operate long distance rail, regional rail, freight services, logistics services, other services, stations, etc. DB is also active overseas and has acquired rail companies and set up operations in 130 countries.

France: The national railway company, SNCF, runs the railways in France through five divisions which separately manage infrastructure, run regional operations, provide long distance and high-speed rail, undertake freight solutions in a multimodal manner and manage stations. It has a global presence in 120 countries through its freight and overseas investments.

Japan: The Japanese rail system was privatized in 1987 when the debts of the Japan National Railways were taken over by a separate corporation and the Japan Railways Group (JR) took over the operations. JR consists of several operating companies which manage the regional systems, and another company that operates freight traffic. Some of these companies have issued shares and are publicly traded. Others are owned by the Japan Railway Construction, Transport and Technology Agency, an independent institution created by an Act of Parliament in 2003 to undertake railway construction projects. JR also owns and operates the shinkansen or bullet trains. The JR group has emerged as a model of good management for rail systems.

The Japanese rail system is a good example of how rail assets can be leveraged to generate profits for both rail and non-rail businesses.

United States of America: The US railway system is overseen by the Federal Railroad Administration. While passenger services are under the National Railroad Passenger Corporation which runs Amtrak, only about 10 per cent of travel is conducted on trains as passengers prefer air and road travel. Hence the major part of the rail system is geared towards freight movement. Freight traffic is undertaken by private operators—classified into three different classes according to their area and value of operations—who also build and maintain railroad tracks.

Unlike the US, India is a long, long away from becoming a country where freight traffic dominates rail transport.

China: A massive rail restructuring plan is underway in the Chinese rail system, following a collision of two high-speed trains in Wenzhou in 2011, which elicited much public approbation. In March 2013, the Ministry of Railways was disbanded and the China Railways Corporation (CRC) was set up. Planning and policy making now rest with the Ministry of Communications. The new State Railways Administration is to function as regulator to monitor technical standards, safety and quality of services. The CRC reports to the top governing body, the State Council, and financial support is to be provided by the Ministry of Finance. The existing eighteen regional railway bureaus will constitute part of the CRC along with their staff of about two million people. The restructuring process is an ongoing effort; thus, the final results of the reformed Chinese rail system, such as how to deal with the huge debt or the manner in which fares will be set, are not yet available.

The Lessons

From the above, it is obvious that there are various models of government and private sector participation across the world. While railways require some form of state intervention, the key aspect in successful models has been the running of the system on a commercial basis with separate organizations for infrastructure, freight and passenger services. Accounting is as per corporate standards and subject to scrutiny as per general corporate regulations. Regulation and operation are entrusted to separate authorities, and administration and management are also vested separately. Funds are raised from the market through the issue of bonds and commercial paper.

Committee Reports

Recognizing that the Indian Railways, too, needs systemic reform, the government set up various committees and groups since the advent of economic liberalization in 1991 to study the challenges faced by the railway system and work out solutions.

The Expert Group on Indian Railways headed by Dr Rakesh Mohan was instituted in July 2001. Its report, 'The Indian Railways Report 2001: Policy Imperatives for Reinvention and Growth', highlights that a successful corporate planning approach to investment programming is required for unlocking necessary funds, and that this can only succeed within a commercial corporate framework. It implies that the introduction of private management for commercial operations of specialized services needs to be seriously considered.

The report is worth examining in detail as it sets out the fundamental guidelines for restructuring the Indian Railways. Meeting its above stated objectives would require basic changes to the functioning of the railways:

- Recasting of the Indian Railways Accounts
- Tariff rebalancing
- Organizational restructuring
- Institutional separation of roles into policy, regulatory and management functions
- Clear differentiation between social obligations and performance imperatives
- Revamping of leadership through the fresh ideas and fresh skills of experts

The Rakesh Mohan Expert Group recommended functioning to be transformed through the following areas:

Vision: The purpose of the Indian Railways has to be clearly defined. The Indian Railways should be seen as a commercial entity that should achieve self-sustaining financial viability.

Strategy: Non-core businesses such as production units, residential colonies, catering, etc. should be spun off.

Governance: Separate institutions for separate roles of policy-making, regulatory and management should be in place. This involves new legislation to mandate changing the Indian Railways into the Indian Railways Corporation.

Structure: Core transportation network may be reorganized into sub-components of freight, passenger, suburban and shared infrastructure; the objective should be to disaggregate into strategic business units.

Commercialization: Accounting should be on a commercial basis in accordance with the Companies Act, which would make it more transparent.

Rebalance pricing: According to the Expert Group, rebalancing of tariffs between passengers and freight and between upper and lower passenger classes is the single most important step in the short term, and should be in line with inflation. It has suggested a clear definition of social and commercial activities, and subsidies to be provided by the government to support social obligations.

According to the report, a market-sensitive approach to pricing will have to be instituted, requiring enhanced organizational skills. Areas where private investments could be introduced include the financing of rolling stock and leasing of wagons, the acquisition and operation of high speed passenger trains and the financing of related rolling stock, freight services in select commodities, and the financing of communication infrastructure, among others.

In the light of increased globalization since the Rakesh Mohan

Group submitted its report, a few other strategies are required to be put in place to improve the functioning of the Indian Railways. For example, there is a proposal to open up selected areas for investments from overseas in the form of foreign direct investment (FDI). Also areas of expansion under implementation and further consideration include Dedicated Freight Corridors (DFC), high-speed passenger rail and urban transport linking to peripheral areas.

In February 2012, the Expert Group for Modernization of the Indian Railways headed by Mr Sam Pitroda brought out its report that laid out the required investments for modernization as ₹5.6 lakh crores over ten years. It recommended that this amount plus additional funding required under the Twelfth Plan be raised through budgetary support, internal generation, borrowings and public-private partnerships. The report made recommendations for modernization of track, signalling, rolling stock and stations. It also suggested time-bound targets for Dedicated Freight Corridors and High Speed Rail Corridors.

Under public-private partnerships, the Group identified a number of areas where private sector investments could be invited, including maintenance and modernization of stations, high-speed rail corridors, elevated trains, manufacturing of rolling stock, power generation, hospitals and schools, etc. Regarding organizational restructuring, the Expert Group suggested reordering the Railway Board on the basis of business functions rather than around cadres. Accounting was also to be revamped along functional lines.

The Twelfth Plan has outlined several major initiatives for the railways during 2012-17, many of which are in line with the recommendations of the above two reports. Completion of the Eastern and Western Dedicated Freight Corridors, covering over 3,000 kilometres, is underway and has made progress, and other DFCs are on the anvil. The focus in the Plan is on the five areas of tracks, bridges, signalling and telecom, rolling stock, and station and freight terminals, with a view towards safety and more efficient railway services. High Speed Rail Corridors and setting up the National High Speed Rail Authority are also part of the Plan.

The Twelfth Plan envisages organizational and accounting changes as well. For correcting the imbalance between passenger and freight traffic, it proposed the setting up of a Rail Tariff Regulatory Authority that has since received approval of the government.

Finally, in the last point of its strategy, the Plan also calls for reorganization of the Indian Railways on business lines, separating non-transportation tasks as well as policy making and operational responsibilities of the Railway Board. This would be the first step towards adopting a corporate culture in the railways.

Current Initiatives

Most of the recommendations of the various committees have been on the table for some time, and some of these have begun to be taken into consideration. For example, the Accounting Reforms Directorate of the Railway Board instituted a project with the Asian Development Bank for improving railway accounts in 2006, for which the final report was submitted in January 2011, and some activity has commenced in selected locations. This project aims to separate accounts for different operations and align it with government accounting standards.

Currently the Rail Budget is presented separately from the general Budget of the central government in a throwback to colonial times when railway procurement and revenues made up a substantial proportion of the overall administrative accounts. If accounting reforms are initiated, this practice would lapse. While a revamp of railway finances is underway, it would also be useful to integrate the railway accounts with the general accounts of the government as with all other ministries and account heads. It may be argued that the finances of an entity with over ₹2 lakh crore worth of Plan expenditure, numerous divisions, and a staff of 1.4 million would be difficult to bring into the overall financing architecture. A closer examination of this would be required and it would form a part of the entire effort to revamp the Indian Railways that should progress without further delay.

Another key initiative has been to set up special purpose vehicles for selected projects or purposes. These operate on commercial lines and have separate accounting. The Dedicated Freight Corridor Corporation of India Ltd. (DFCCIL), the Konkan Railway Corporation, IRCON, RITES, etc. are public sector corporations functioning under the Ministry of Railways.

Public-private partnership or PPP has been progressively extended, although the level of investment is still very low. The Railway Budget of 2013-14 envisaged an investment of ₹63,363 crores of which ₹6,000 crores was expected to come from the private sector, a significant step-up from estimates for earlier years, which stood at less than ₹2,000 crores. However, the success in PPP has not been as expected. For example, although private participation was permitted in CONCOR (Container Corporation of India Ltd.), the results have been disappointing due to issues relating to pricing and sharing of revenues.

> Public-private partnership or PPP has been progressively extended, although the level of investment is still very low.

It is important to build greater confidence in PPP and to attract private investments, as without the involvement of private companies, the Indian Railways will not be able to garner the funds required for modernization and expansion. The private sector is also expected to bring in better managerial and accounting practices, leading to increased cost competitiveness and efficiency in the railway system.

Private players look for a more consultative approach in developing major projects where they are expected to engage. Investors must be assured of a level playing field so that a real competition between them as well as between private and Indian Railways entities can be promoted. The entire PPP approach needs to move from a licence-based regime to investments for non-end users. Freight savings and investment returns need to be linked to improved technology and efficiency.

The Indian Railways has set up a PPP Cell to promote private participation that identifies specific projects, recommends appropriate models and interacts with stakeholders for better policies. During the Eleventh Plan, private investments stood at around 4 per cent of the Plan outlay for railways.

Managing Change

Rail transport services, being an inherent monopoly, have the tendency to suffer from a number of ailments, compounded over the years. These range from financial ills and rising subsidies, resulting from irrational pricing decisions, to high costs, low efficiency and low productivity. The result is that services are inadequately available and over-stretched, quality is poor, and customer requirements are not met. Infrastructure maintenance and creation becomes a huge challenge in this scenario, as the investments needed are simply out of reach. The poor levels of maintenance ultimately lead to safety issues.[23]

The above issues have led to different models of workings being adopted by different countries. When it comes to railways, there is a compelling case for adopting professional business management practices, which would clearly demarcate the government's social and commercial roles. This would enable better management with cost competitiveness and higher productivity, provide streamlined customer services, and better employee satisfaction. It would also allow railways to capture a larger share in the movement of passengers and goods, and become the most efficient and clean mode of transport.

Most importantly, by inducing greater efficiency, productivity and cost competitiveness into the system, the needs of the general railway traveller, in terms of services, affordability, and accessibility can be met. Also, a more competitive transport mode would lower the cost of final goods for the consumer. Under the current scenario, the financial burden of the railways on the exchequer is likely to erode future passenger and freight services.

The first challenge would be the reorganization of the railways. The Indian Railways represents a massive and complex organizational structure under the Ministry of Railways. A minister and two ministers of state are in charge, supported by the Railway Board headed by a chairman. Members of the Railway Board look after various functional responsibilities including electrical, staff, engineering, mechanical and traffic responsibilities, along with a

---

[23]Further reading—'The Restructuring of the Railways', United Nations Economic and Social Commission for Asia and the Pacific (UNESCAP), 2003 http://www.unescap.org/ttdw/Publications/TIS_pubs/RailwayRestructuring/RailwayRestructuring.pdf

financial commissioner. The Board additionally consists of one secretary, a director-general for health and a director-general for the Railway Protection Force. The system is divided into seventeen zones, each headed by a General Manager. The production centres of the Indian Railways include Chittaranjan Locomotive Works, Diesel Locomotive Works, Integral Coach Factory, Rail Coal Factory and Rail Wheel Factory, among others. There are sixteen public sector undertakings or public sector enterprises such as the IRFC, IRCTC, RVNL, etc., which come under the ministry.

Second, separation of accounts of the different operations would not be an easy task, given the multiple interconnecting operations of the railways. The total earnings of the Indian Railways in 2012-13 stood at close to ₹1.24 lakh crore, with passenger earnings at ₹31,000 crores and goods revenue at ₹85,000 crores. Ordinary working expenses amounted to over ₹84,000 crores, and it placed about ₹21,000 crores in pension fund.

Third, the question of social responsibility of the railways in providing affordable and accessible transport for millions of people at low-income levels would have to be worked out. As mentioned earlier, cost of tickets is the primary consideration for travellers, and higher tickets would place train journeys out of the reach of many people. In other countries, government subsidy to rail services operated by private companies can be extensive. In the US, the tracks built and operated by freight companies are made available to Amtrak and the government paid $1.4 billion to Amtrak as subsidy in 2011.[24] In the UK, the government paid operators £ 4 billion in 2011, at the rate of 7.5 pence per mile travelled.[25] The Indian

---

[24]'Amtrak's True Costs', *The Economist*, 7 Nov 2011, http://www.economist.com/blogs/gulliver/2011/11/road-v-rail

[25]'How Much is Your Train Subsidised?', BBC News, 11 October 2012, http://www.bbc.co.uk/news/business-19914219

passenger service loss currently works out to more than $ 4 billion.

Fourth, the construction of future infrastructure requirements as well as the investment in modernization requires a huge amount of funds. The Pitroda Committee estimated that approximately $40 billion of gross budgetary support would be needed to meet the modernization endeavour, expected to cost over $125 billion (including expenditure under the Twelfth Plan) over the next five years. Just catering to these requirements would be a big deterrent to effective change.

At present, the government is expecting the route of public-private partnership to fund a large part of the development of the railways. However, such a large private sector investment amount is not expected in other countries, and it is unlikely that in the absence of clear and transparent guidelines, private industry would be able to meet these expectations. As per the Twelfth Plan, about a quarter of investments are envisaged from the private sector, which appears unreasonable.

Five, streamlining the various ways in which the railway hires its managerial, professional and technical staff. About 1.3 million people work directly in the Indian Railways, in Groups A, B, C and D. Recruitment for the Group A staff is either through the civil services examinations or through the Indian Engineering Services or through the Special Class Railway Apprentices' Examination. The Allied Services stream, which is open to graduates of any discipline, includes the Indian Railway Traffic Services, the Indian Railway Accounts Services, the Indian Railway Personnel Services and the Railway Protection Force. Recruitment for other groups is through different selection systems. There are separate services for medical staff, railway protection, railway stores, mechanical engineers and electrical engineers. Apart from this, railway unions are a potent force.

On the other hand, employees of the railways comprise a rich talent reservoir and enjoy specialized experiences that may not be available in any other industry. Any systemic change would require bringing on board these diverse sections of employees while also successfully merging them into the new entity or entities.

The Track Ahead

It is not easy to unravel an entity as humongous as the Indian Railways and reorder it as per different business norms and regulations. The global preference is for a business model of functioning, and as the experiences of different countries indicate, it is a doable task. Most recently, China has undertaken a complete revamping of the organization of its railways by disbanding its Ministry of Railways and setting up a corporation.

India, too, would ultimately need to do likewise, in line with global models that have worked. Expectations from a modern and smooth functioning railway system must be clearly defined and its objectives must be outlined. A consultative and participatory approach would be required for this as any restructuring effort would raise multiple objections from various quarters. However, it must also be recognized that inordinate delays would place the Indian railway system further behind its peers, which is unacceptable given the current scenario of collapsing technology adaptation.

The Indian Railways has traversed a remarkable journey since its inception in 1853. It has unified a nation and placed it on track. It has enabled rapid social and economic transformation of the country and accelerated its path to development. Today, the Indian Railways must once again reprise its glory and emerge as the artery of the nation.

SPACE—TIME CONVERGENCE AND THE URBANIZATION OF INDIA

Seema Sharma

The concept of space and time as a human experience, the world over, was transformed by the arrival of the railways. Considered largely a symbol of the industrial revolution, the railways not only helped the spread of industrialization across the world, but also 'annihilated' the concept of space and time for ordinary people. Commodities moved at faster speeds—and so did people. Even ideas were carried faster, to greater distances than ever before, giving people greater access to news and views. This proved to be the undoing of the local character of the small towns and villages that the railway traversed.

Redefining Distances

The railways, during the process of their construction, reshaped geographies, geologies and created new histories. Going up and down inclines or gradients—even eliminating them when required—tunnelling through mountains, bridging rivers, streams and gorges, the railways took on and conquered every natural contour that stood in its way.

Railways transformed the landscape, and as a result they simultaneously transformed the way travellers experienced the countryside. It was the visuals outside the train that were commented upon by sociologists and litterateurs alike. Victor Hugo, during one of his train travels, in 1837, described a view from a train window as such: 'the towns, the steeples, and the trees perform a crazy, mingling dance,' causing sociologist George Simmel to call 'this multiplication of visual impressions' 'nervous fatigue'. This is also the sort of sensation that is felt nowadays in urban areas.

The railways thus bequeathed India with a new geography. Spaces were now enlarged; scope of travel magnified; pilgrimages—a great passion and one of the earliest tourist industries in India—could now be undertaken as holy places were now accessible. The space–time convergence through the railways in India was immensely beneficial as well as a huge drawback. Increased travel to pilgrimage spots changed the existing economies. The railways would now be catering to an increased number of people and huge profits could be made from it.

The flip side was the obliteration of local character of isolated towns and villages, and with it the sense of alienation amongst people started emerging. With the railways, speed ruled leading to a space–time convergence. Industries were consolidated and consequently traditional activities were sacrificed at the altar of strategically and economically viable rail routes for the British.

Although the railways were regarded as a tangible, larger than life British institution, it still gave early travellers in India a feeling of unease. For example: On 23 August 1854, the *Bengal Hukaru* reported: 'One Roop Chand Ghose, a flourishing dealer in piece goods and perfumery, when set down at the end of his journey from Howrah to Hoogly, felt strongly suspicious at the short time it had taken, and went down the street asking people the name of the place he was at. It took a long time before conviction gained upon him that verily he had come to Hoogly.'

Another story in the same paper: 'Pandit Ranalunkur Banerjee, after duly consulting the stars undertook his trip to Hoogly but declined to take the return journey because he said that 'too much travelling on the car of fire was calculated to shorten life'. Seeing that it annihilates time and space and curtails the length of every other journey, it must shorten the 'journey of human life.'

Industrialization and Urbanization

Although the railways were simultaneously the product and the driver of industrialization in Europe and elsewhere in the world, they failed to industrialize India until after Independence, in spite of the fact that 59,000 kilometres of tracks had already been laid. This belied Karl Marx's view that the advent of railways would speed up industrialization in India. Though there was some industrialization brought about by the railways such as the mining, textile and a small amount of engineering industries, it was insignificant when compared to the large-scale industrialization that happened in Europe and the North American continent.

A consequence of industrialization was the joint processes of urbanization and modernization that were brought about by technology in the form of railways. Production and efficiency increased and the speedy movement of merchandise led to the availability of a greater range of consumer goods. These were now no more a part of the local identity of a place as the railway created a definite spatial distance between their production point and the destination of their consumption. The commodity at its place of consumption attains its value.

The railways also played a vital role in urbanization. As new zones to visit were defined, large-scale migrations, temporary or permanent, were now possible. Thus, a wave of migrants rode the rails to urban centres to seek their fortunes. Away from their villages, inherited, traditional spaces, they merged with the unique culture of the urban centres. In fact, urbanization for migrants starts the moment they board a train, come into contact with different cultures, communities, belief-systems to ultimately shed lifelong traditions.

Because of the railways temporary communities are formed in urban areas where spaces are shrunk to bring communities closer. Cities merge into one another—for example, Delhi-Jaipur, the expansion of Jaipur towards Ajmer, Mumbai into Panvel into Navi Mumbai, all moving along the lines of the expanding railway network. It is as if urban centres are spreading their tentacles through new railway lines to bring rural areas into their fold. The time taken to reach another place shortens; cities are no longer self-contained areas; they spread uncontrollably.

The railways destroy the traditional time–space continuum even today as it continues to be one of the fastest modes of transport. Earlier, the railways allowed suburbs to grow into satellite towns but its expansion is now consuming them. India is swiftly moving towards urbanization with provincial cities like Ghaziabad, Ludhiana, Meerut, Muzaffarnagar stretching along the existing railway lines. In fact, currently the projects that Indian Railways are working on include expansion of the suburban systems in metropolises that will inevitably expand the reach of different cities. There are huge investment plans for Metro Railways in Kolkata, Mumbai, Chennai and a 101.05-kilometre multi-model transport system in Hyderabad.

In Europe, most of the railway stations are on the outskirts of the city. Goods and people would come and be carried into the city through other modes of transport such as roadways. In India, however, the railway stations were built in the heart of the city.

Vast areas were and still are being used to construct stations, along with business centres to service the commerce connected with the railways. The railways brought both the goods and customers to the city, and gradually activity coalesced around the station and they became magnets for the developing city. Roads developed but only as feeders to the main transportation hub.

India's urban share in 1951 was 17 per cent. It went up to 31 per cent in 2011—a two-fold increase. In 1951 India had only 5 cities with a population of over one million. Today there are 56 such cities with three having more than 10 million people each. This is the inevitable outcome of economic growth, which is characterized by the transition from a rural-agrarian to urban-industrial services led economy. The growing railway network has shrunk space by increasing possibility of migration from rural to urban areas.

Since 1950-51, the number of originating passengers on Indian Railways has gone up from 1,284 million annually to 8,224 million passengers in 2011-12, an eight-fold increase. This increased passenger movement indicates a collaborative relationship between movement and settlement in urban areas. In 1950-51, a person was travelling on an average 51.8 kilometres whereas by 2011-12, the average distance travelled had gone up to 127.2 kilometres. The railways is the most popular form of long distance travel today and is also gaining popularity as an important intra–city mode of travel. Thus urbanization today is two pronged—one led by migration from rural to urban areas and the other led by the growth of a small city into a big city.

People living in Maharashtra constitute 13.5 per cent of India's urban population followed by Uttar Pradesh at 11.8 per cent and Tamil Nadu at 9.3 per cent. If we juxtapose this with the route kilometres of rail track in these states, we get the following results: UP leads with 13.7 per cent of total route kilometres (this is also attributable to its size), Maharashtra follows with 8.6 per cent and

Tamil Nadu trails at 6.1 per cent. The only other states having more route kilometres than Tamil Nadu are Gujarat, Rajasthan and Madhya Pradesh.

In the past decade, the number of train kilometres has increased from 397 million to 605 million (non-suburban), an increase of 34.3 per cent. Also in the past decade, the growth of smaller cities has been at the rate of 40 per cent leading us to believe in the population explosion which is evident from the fact that India's 340 million urban population is expected to rise to 590 million by 2030 according to reports by McKinsey. These are telling figures.

The easy accessibility lent by the railways, the speeds of its travel, shrinking spaces, facilitates and accelerates urbanization. The train tracks coming into the city meet with the tracks radiating out of the railway stations.

Indian Railways is in itself a big industry employing 14 lakh people. Announcement of a survey of a new-line, granting a stoppage to an important train in a small town, setting up a workshop or a plant leads to a buzz and generation of employment opportunities. The growth of that city/town is ensured. Even though the rail share of traffic has reduced when compared to road, the ongoing projects of Dedicated Freight corridors and the High Speed corridors will only enhance the speed of urbanization of India.

Select References

Schivelbusch, Wolfgang, *The Railway Journey: Industrialization of Time and Space in the 19th century* (1977, Berkley, University of California)
Indian Railways Yearbook 2011–2012 (2012, Indian Railways)
Srinivasan, Tiwari, Silas, eds., *Our Indian Railway: Themes in India's Railway History* (2006, Foundation Books)
Dutta, Arup Kumar, *Indian Railway: The Final Frontier* (2002, Indian Railways)
www.McKinsey.com/insights/urbanisation
Kerr, Ian J., ed., *Railways in Modern India (Oxford in India Readings: Themes in Indian History)* (2001, Oxford University Press India, New Delhi)

Photograph courtesy: Rail Bandhu *Magazine*

When the Train Came to Deyra Dhoon
Ruskin Bond

The Winding Path to Bhutan
Omair Ahmad

On Board the Bombay Express
Shoba Narayan

Aboard the Vivek Express
Aasheesh Sharma

Changing Lanes
Kartik Iyengar

Kangra: The Land of the White Mountain
Premola Ghose

Part 2
RAIL TRAVELOGUES

WHEN THE TRAIN CAME TO DEYRA DHOON

Ruskin Bond

In the forest, the animals raised their heads as a strange sound assailed their ears.

It was dawn, and the jungle was coming to life. A sambhar belled. A leopard coughed. A tiger yawned and said: 'Aa-oonh!' A herd of spotted deer streamed across a forest clearing. A peacock shrieked. A wild boar grunted, wanting breakfast. Then that strange sound again, almost like an elephant trumpeting. But the elephants did not like it. They stamped their feet, annoyed, and raised their trunks and signalled defiance. Between the elephants and the approaching monster there would always be trouble.

It was daybreak and a crisp December morning, and the night train from Delhi was on its inaugural run, panting and snorting as it took the final incline before its swift descent into the valley of 'Deyra Dhoon'—for that was how the town was spelt in the year 1900, when the first train came thundering into the valley.

The animals were perturbed by the hoot and whistle of the approaching steam engine; but they were not the only ones to be taken by surprise. The villagers from Raiwala and Doiwala and Harrawala streamed out of their houses to wave and gesticulate and marvel at this huffing, puffing wonder that was going to change their lives.

A few years earlier, the trains had come as far as Saharanpur and Ambala, soon to be busy junctions. A mountain railway, burrowing through a hundred tunnels, had opened up Simla to the rest of the country. And now, to the east, lines were being laid through the forests of the Terai, to Lhaksar and Hardwar, Kathgodam and Kotdwar, making the hills more accessible. Dehradun would become the railhead for Mussourie, uncrowned 'queen of the hills'. (Simla was the summer capital, the haunt of Viceroys and phantom rickshaws; Mussoorie in spite of its many churches—or because of them—was for fun and frolic and the occasional scandal, and therefore equally important.)

> The animals were perturbed by the hoot and whistle of the approaching steam engine.

Soon that December morning, the sun came up with its usual splendour, first as a crimson glow on the horizon, then a gentle parting of the valley's mist, and finally a glorious onslaught on field and forest and human habitation; and the little railway station, receiving a passenger train for the first time, came to life with a burst of music as the band of the Gurkha Regiment struck up a familiar air.

Some seventy years before, at the conclusion of the Anglo-Nepalese War during which fierce battles had been fought in the Doon and in the hills of Kumaon, Garhwal and Sirmur, the disbanded Gurkha soldiers had been taken into the army of British India and had proved their mettle in Afghanistan, Burma and beyond. Dehra was the home of the regiment, which boasted a band that had played at many a parade and polo match at bases as distant as Cyprus and Malta.

The regiment's present commandant, Colonel Shakespeare, was popular with the troops. For many years he had wanted a son, and one of his soldiers had suggested that he perform a puja in the temple in the Gurkha lines. This he had done, earning for himself the sobriquet of Devi Sahib. A son was born. In time, the little boy romped about in the Gurkha lines, where he was popularly known as Devi Sahib ka chhokra. Now three, he stood restlessly beside his parents on the Dehradun railway platform, while the band struck up tune after familiar tune: 'D'ye Ken John Peel'; 'Loch Lomond'; 'Comin' Thru' the Rye'; 'Rule Britannia'; and by way of relief, a popular number straight from the London music-halls: 'Has Anybody Seen Our Nelly?'

The little boy wanted to run off and play, but was held in check by his mother.

'Shh!' she said. 'The Train is coming. Can you hear it?'

It was difficult to hear anything above the wail of the bagpipes, but presently there was a loud hoot and a prolonged whistle, and the band stopped playing. Before it could start off again, there was another blast of the engine's hooter, a roar from the small crowd on the platform, a whoosh of air, a trembling of the rails. And then, like a dragon of old, the red-and-gold steam engine burst through the receding mist, into the sunshine, gliding to a stop beside the decorated platform.

Stationmaster Mukherjee dashed about on the platform, unable to contain his excitement. 'It's here, it's here, the Doon Express, God bless us all!' Mr Mukherjee, a good-natured man, was always showering blessings on people. It was also rumoured that he wrote poetry in secret.

Colonel Shakespeare, although distantly related to his namesake, did not write poetry, but was engaged in penning a history of the Gurkha Wars and recent military engagements in Afghanistan and Burma. His wife was writing a cook book—*Custards, Jellies and Jams in a Hot Climate.*

There were a number of other VIPs on the platform—a magistrate, a railway superintendent, a nawab from Purkazi and a raja from Bijnor—and several on the train, including a well-known big-game hunter. But we are concerned here with a certain gentleman, very English-looking, in tweeds and plus fours and wearing a deer-stalker hat in the manner of Sherlock Holmes—an English country gentleman about to make the rounds of his estates.

Which was exactly what he was about to do.

For this was Cecil D. Lincoln, Esq., proprietor of Lucknow's palatial Carlton Hotel, and part owner of Darjeeling's Everest Hotel and Calcutta's Great Eastern. He was in his mid-thirties, balding slightly, and tall, but with a slight stoop acquired after years of bending to negotiate entrances and exits that had been designed for smaller men. Now on his way to Mussoorie to open a new hotel, he had already made a note to the effect that all doors must be large enough to allow both the tall and the broad to pass through comfortably.

Two years previously, the old Mussoorie school, Maddock's, had closed down, its owners having run into debt and then lost all their savings and assets when the Alliance Bank collapsed. Lincoln had snapped up the school's extensive buildings and spacious grounds for a song. He had spent much more on renovations and restructuring. The buildings were almost ready, and over the winter months they would be furnished, redesigned, decorated. The gilded gateway already displayed the name of the hotel: The Savoy.

It would open in April, before the start of the summer season.

As Mr Lincoln descended from his railway carriage, a swarm of barefoot porters surged forward, eager to handle his luggage. On earlier visits, when he arrived in Dehra by the horse-drawn coach from Saharanpur (at least two sturdy stallions were needed to pull the carriage up the steep incline of the Mohand Pass), he had always carried plenty of luggage and was a generous tipper. Now, while the porters took care of his trunks and holdalls, he stepped forward and introduced himself to Colonel Shakespeare and the others.

There were not a great many passengers on this inaugural train. Most of them had got down at Hardwar. Dehradun was still a very small town. But in the summer months, holiday-makers—British and Anglo-Indian and the more prosperous Indian families—would head for the hill station, and then the train would be full.

Stationmaster Mukherjee had laid out a sumptuous breakfast for his special guests, and this was served in the newly opened Refreshment Room, where a portrait of a plump and ageing Queen Victoria gazed sternly down at her subjects. It did not affect anyone's appetite, and as most of those assembled had so far only had their chhota-hazri, mere tea and biscuits, they were fully prepared to take on the barra-hazri: tea, toast, eggs boiled or scrambled, or half-boiled in egg cups, more toast, marmalade, a local jam, tomato chutney, more toast and a second cup of tea thank you. They fell upon it with enthusiasm.

Mr Mukherjee had heard that Englishmen liked kippers with their breakfast. 'What's a kipper?' he had asked an Anglo-Indian engine-driver. 'It's a fish, I think,' the driver had said, 'but you won't find it in our rivers.' Mr Mukherjee had thought of serving up sardines, but they weren't available either. Not to be discouraged, he had the local fishermen bring him a supply of tiny mountain trout, and these were deep fried and served with tomato sauce. Unfortunately, these little fish contained a multitude of tiny bones, barely visible but ever-present. The magistrate's wife choked on one, couldn't stop coughing, went into convulsions and collapsed in a planter's armchair. It was her good fortune that the local surgeon, Dr Butcher, was next to her. He turned lazily in his chair and considered her for a long moment, as if deciding if he should bother. Finally, he stuck one fat finger down her throat and removed the offending fish-bone, almost throttling the lady to death in the process.

Dr Butcher then returned to his breakfast. He had a voracious appetite and attacked his food ferociously, as though it were an enemy he had to defeat. In ten minutes he demolished five buttered toasts, six boiled eggs, and three 'kippers', bones and all. Meanwhile, young master Shakespeare, Devi Sahib's chhokra, had broken two egg cups and polished off the marmalade.

The train, the station, the breakfast, were all pronounced a great success, and the company dispersed in good humour. Only Mr Lincoln remained on the platform, surveying his belongings which had been arranged in a heap in the middle of the platform. Something was missing.

'Where's the piano?' he asked.

At that moment two struggling porters emerged from a rear compartment, bringing out a handsome new piano, which nearly lost a leg as it crash-landed on the platform.

'A beautiful instrument!' exclaimed Mr Mukherjee. 'Do you perform on it, sir?'

'No, I'm tone deaf. It's for the hotel. Next summer we'll open with a grand ball. I've engaged Jack Hilton and his orchestra for the season. But we must have our own piano. The trouble is—how do we get it up the mountain? There's no train to Mussoorie, and no motor road as yet.'

Mr Mukherjee considered the problem. 'There *is* a train, sir,' he said with a smile. 'It's called the "Bullock-Cart" train. It's run by Mr Bohle and his Brewery. He won't charge much, provided you place a good order for his beer.'

'Is it any good, the beer?'

'Terrible stuff. But the soldiers up in Landour drink it. They don't have a choice, Solan being too far away.'

'Up there they'd be better off with some rum from Rosa. But we'll do our best to please Mr Bohle. The Savoy will need everyone's good wishes,' said Mr Lincoln.

Soon after, Lincoln was in a buggy to Rajpur, where a sturdy Deccan pony waited to take him up the steep bridle road to Mussoorie.

THE WINDING PATH TO BHUTAN

Omair Ahmad

In 2005 I met a most interesting man, Michael Rutland, who was just returning from England after being awarded the Order of the British Empire by Queen Elizabeth II in the Christmas Honours list. Many people earn such laurels, few physics teachers do so, and even fewer such teachers have been tutors to future kings. The really interesting thing about Michael was that, in 1970, he had been tutor to Jigme Singye Wangchuck, who would go on to be the fourth King of Bhutan, ruling for thirty-six years until he abdicated in favour of his son in 2006. Michael's father, too, had been an interesting man, a minister in Chiang Kai Shak's Koumintang government until he was sent to Oxford to study agriculture. It was at Oxford that Michael's parents had met, and parted, when his father returned home to battle the Communist onslaught.

Michael had served in Britain's Royal Air Force, and after his first tour, decided to become a physics teacher. A few years into his career he was recruited to be tutor to the then Crown Prince of Bhutan, and as a lark as much as anything else, he said yes.

I was keen to write his story; he was keen that I write on Bhutan. We decided that I would visit at least, but the idea stayed just that, an idea, until two years later. My job as a journalist paid peanuts, and the flight to Bhutan was expensive—although it did have the allure of flying near Mount Everest, and the third highest mountain in the world, and the fourth, and the fifth. I was saving up for the trip, when a close friend of mine, Mandavi, returned to India from the US and over the course of a telephone conversation I mentioned that I was thinking of visiting Bhutan. She exclaimed in delight that she was born there, and told me to abandon the idea of flying there. 'The closest railway stop is at New Jalpaiguri, and from there you take the road to the border town of Phuentsholing. After that, it takes a few hours from there to drive to Thimphu. The rail journey and the road trip are equally stunning. I envy you the trip. It's been so long since I've visited.'

For me there was a lovely symmetry to it all. My first trips to the mountains were also mediated by the railways. My boarding school, which I joined when I was twelve years old, was in Mussoorie, and my trips to and from there involved a long journey by rail. I would board a train from Gorakhpur, my home town, to go to Lucknow, and from there switch trains to Dehradun. Most importantly, after a couple of years, I was allowed to travel alone.

I cannot tell you how liberating that was. I had my hiking bag and maybe a small suitcase, and that was all. During the journey there were many cups of tea, and the samosas at the Gonda railway station were among the snacks I used to make sure to wake up for. Through it all, I would have a book, something bought from the Wheeler bookstore at a railway station, and once I was older, even a Walkman, to keep me company. The book was read slowly, with many a break to look out at the rolling green fields of the Gangetic plains, or to doze as the train clickety-clacked its way across the country.

Over the years this love of the long journey by train has led me to construct a 'travelling carapace', and this was the exoskeleton I had on when I arrived at the New Delhi railway station that December day in 2007 to make the first leg of my journey to Bhutan. It consisted, first of all, of a bit of stubble. I hated travelling clean-shaven. To this was added a pair of comfortable boots, an old pair of jeans, my leather jacket and a cap whose shade covered the top of my face and left my eyes in shadow. Since it was winter, the leather jacket was reinforced by a fleece and a thick cotton shirt. Over all of this was my hiking bag and a shoulder bag.

Each little piece added one more shade of distance between me and the rest of the world, the final piece being the distance of music. Previous Walkmans have been replaced by a small iPod, and I was completely insulated from the world, if I wished to be.

I was not able to board the train on my first trip to the railway station. Having come very early in the morning, I was told that the train had been delayed because of a derailment further along the route, so I returned to come back at a more decent hour, like a few thousand others. New Delhi railway station was frighteningly crowded. There were people from all walks of life milling around. My carapace shielded me, all the layers keeping people at a distance, and the hiking bag weighed me down so that I was not swept off course as I made my way towards Platform Number 12.

Turning back at the head of the stairs before I descended down to the platform, I made a rough calculation. Counting the number of people in a row and multiplying it by the number of rows in front of me, I guessed there were at least fifteen hundred people before me descending the stairs, carrying all forms of luggage, some on their heads, some slung under their arms, others dragging their suitcases behind them. Taking a deep breath, I plunged down the stairs, wondering at the back of my mind what a Bhutanese would make of this. Thimphu, the most populous dzonkhag, or district, had a population of just about a hundred thousand, with a density of fifty-four people per square kilometre. Gasa, the least populous, had a population density of one person per kilometre. In contrast, Delhi had a population of about fourteen million, with more than nine thousand people per square kilometre.

I could not imagine how a Bhutanese would react, but the thought of mountains, of free air, made me deeply nostalgic. It reminded me of the six years of my childhood spent in a boarding school in the foothills of the Himalaya, situated at a little over six thousand feet above sea level, around the same height as Thimphu, the capital of Bhutan. The memory did not help me relax, only serving to heighten my claustrophobia, so I did the one thing I could: plugged in my earphones and took out one of the two books that I had put aside for the long train ride to New Jalpaiguri.

The first book was by Jamie Zeppa, titled, *Beyond the Earth and the Sky*. The name came from a translation of an expression of gratitude in Bhutanese, 'I am thankful to you beyond the earth and sky'. Jamie's book was an account of her travelling from Canada to eastern Bhutan at the age of twenty-three to be a volunteer teacher in the eastern region of Trashigang in the late 1980s, and her engagement with the country, her students, and Buddhism. The story was immensely interesting, and I was lost for an hour until the train came, and it was time for me to board.

I made my way to my train coach to look at the reservation chart pasted near the entrance. I had been assigned a berth in the 'Reserved Against Cancellation' category. This means that I had side-berth that must be shared with somebody else. In the normal course of things I would not have been too concerned. A side-berth can be folded up to make it into two individual seats, which are quite comfortable on their own. For a shorter journey it would have been all right, but it was fifteen hundred kilometres to my stop, a distance that the train was scheduled to cover in almost thirty hours. I had no wish to spend the time sitting, even if it was by a window.

For a moment I was overcome with the temptation to call it all off, but it passed. I was travelling in an air-conditioned coach. At least I would not be among the thousands that I had seen on the platform. As a child I had travelled in rougher situations, and an A/C coach was far superior to those days—although I must say I missed the open windows, the wind, and the tea and pakora sellers at every station.

I decided to rely on my carapace and, upon finding my seat, barricaded myself with my bags, and plunged aggressively into Zeppa's book. Two hours later I reluctantly lowered my guard when the Ticket Examiner arrived. I removed one earphone.

'Your berth has been confirmed,' he told me.

'What?' I was pretty far down the list, and could not believe my luck.

'Your berth has been confirmed,' he repeated, a note of irritation creeping into his voice. The other person sharing the side-berth had already started to move his belongings to where he, too, had been given a full-berth.

I was thankful beyond the earth and sky, and finished Jamie's book, my legs stretched out to their full length.

■

It was late morning the next day when I woke up. Or at least, when I decided to rise. I had overheard bits of conversation and they revealed that I had a full day ahead of me. The train had been delayed again and again through the night, stopping in the middle of nowhere as other trains swooshed past. There was a report of a bomb blast on the Rajdhani Express that had left ahead of us in the same direction. Nobody knew who was responsible for the bomb but it was assumed that one of the militant groups that infest India's northeastern states had a hand in it. There were a number of army and paramilitary personnel in the coach, and they exchanged their bit of gossip. Tea-sellers came and went. Despite the delay, it did not seem as if anybody was too upset.

I rose, stretched, cleaned up, and went to stand by the door. The train was stopped somewhere that had no sign, and some of us got down to stretch our legs. It always amazes me to see how green, vast and lovely India is—an experience that we forget in the cars we drive in our cities, or the flights we take between them. Maybe it is the reason that train journeys remain such a joy still. Then the whistle blew in warning, and we scrambled back into the train, and I found myself another book.

It was titled *A Certain Ambiguity*, and co-written by Gaurav Suri and Hartosh Bal, childhood friends with a love of mathematics. I had attended the book launch shortly before my trip to Bhutan, and Hartosh had autographed my book by writing, '$a+b^n/n = x$ therefore God exists'. Laughing at the look on my face he told me about the famous anecdote involving the Swiss mathematician Leonhard Euler. Euler is considered one of the greatest mathematicians of all time, and he spent much of his time in the Russian court of Catherine the Great. Once, the philosopher and encyclopaedist, Denis Diderot, was visiting. The empress, happy enough with the fame of Diderot, was disturbed by his atheistic leanings and felt that his heretical thoughts would influence members of her court. So she ordered Euler to confront Diderot.

Euler agreed, and the message was passed on to Diderot that a mathematician had produced a proof of the existence of God. Diderot readily agreed to hear the proof, and at court was confronted by Euler who said, in a tone of complete confidence, 'Sir, $a+b^n/n = x$ therefore God exists; respond.'

The mathematical statement is nonsense, but it was said with such bravado that Diderot fell into confusion and left Russia in his embarrassment.

Hartosh and Gaurav's book told the story of an Indian mathematician, charged under blasphemy laws in the US during the 1920s, arguing with a judge about how the rigour of mathematics should be used to prove or disprove the validity of religion. Much of the book was about the pure joy that mathematicians, across the ages, have taken in the pursuit of the truth, toppling many assumptions along the way, both within and outside the field of mathematics. I wondered how much the advent of modern education had impacted the myths of Bhutan.

> Diderot readily agreed to hear the proof, and at court was confronted by Euler who said, in a tone of complete confidence, 'Sir, $a + b^n/n = x$ therefore God exists; respond.'

These things are hard to gauge, especially from the outside. It was evening again, and I made my way to the end of the carriage and the doorway so that I could look outside at the dark countryside rolling by, interrupted by sudden spattering of lights in the distance indicating some habitation or other. Looking up, I was pleased to see Orion the Hunter riding high in the sky. That particular constellation was an old friend. This might just have been because Orion is quite large and easy to spot. When I first fell in love with physics as a child, astronomy became a particular interest and constellations were among the first things I learnt about, spotting them in the clear night skies.

What I remembered about the stories woven around the constellation is from a book on Greek mythology from my school library. The story went that Artemis, the goddess of the hunt, fell in love with Orion, the greatest of mortal hunters. Her brother, offended that his sister could love a mere mortal, sent various beasts to kill Orion but the hunter overcame them all. In the end a giant scorpion, a pet of Diana's brother, was sent to battle Orion. Although Orion was able to kill the scorpion, he, too, died from the poison of the scorpion's sting.

Bhutan, too, is littered with such tales: of the monastery that was chained down to the earth so that it wouldn't fly away, of the marks of Guru Rimpoche's passage to be found in various rock formations and other natural phenomenon. No doubt there shall be a number of scientific explanations found for many of them, but I wondered what impact, if any, science would have on the faith of the people in the country. I learned about the substance of the stars before I read the story of Artemis, and the belief system that manufactured the story withered away more than a thousand years ago. The story still retained its power, and I gathered some comfort looking up at Orion, on this train to the border of a country I had never visited, knowing full well the explanations that the natural sciences have provided us, but enjoying the mystery still.

ON BOARD THE BOMBAY EXPRESS

Shoba Narayan

The most important thing when travelling by train in India is not whether you have a seat in first class (more comfortable) or second class (more congenial), whether you have confirmed tickets, or even your destination. The most important thing is the size of your neighbour's tiffin carrier, the Indian lunch box. If you are lucky, you will be seated near a generous Marwari matron whose way of making your acquaintance is to hand you a hot roti stuffed with potato saag.

I was fourteen when this happened to me, and I still remember biting into the soft, ghee-stained roti and feeling the explosion of spices in my mouth as I encountered cumin, coriander, ginger, green chillies, pungent onions and finally—like a sigh—comfortably soft potato. It was dawn. The train whistled mournfully as it click-clacked its way through the misty countryside. A cool breeze wafted through the open window and teased the curls behind my ear. Fragrant turmeric-yellow saag dribbled from the corner of my mouth. A perfect symphony for the senses.

It was 1981, and my family and I were taking the Bombay Express from Madras to Bombay (now officially called Chennai and Mumbai) for our annual summer vacation, a trip of about thirty hours. Across from me, my parents, still faint and groggy from the effort of packing and bundling us on to the train, were nodding off. Beside me, my thirteen-year-old pest of a brother was elbowing for the window seat, which I had no intention of relinquishing. I turned towards the Marwari matron hopefully. She smiled as she opened another container. In a trance, I went to her.

Marwaris are from the desert state of Rajasthan, and Marwari women are known to be fantastic cooks. They are also known to be generous to a fault, which makes them dream companions for a long train journey. Enterprising Gujaratis, on the other hand, were more businesslike, which meant that I had to ingratiate myself to gain access to their divine kadi (sweet-and-sour buttermilk soup). A boisterous Punjabi family was always good for card games interspersed with hearty rajma (spiced kidney beans). Intellectual Bengalis from Calcutta, now called Kolkata, were a challenge. I had to match wits with them before they would share their luscious roshogollas (sweet cheese balls) and sandesh (milk and sugar squares) with me. I didn't bother with the South Indians, being one myself.

It was this glorious home-cooked food that made the train journeys of my childhood memorable. My uncle in Bangalore (now Bengaluru) was a few hours away by the Lal Bagh Express; my grandparents were an overnight journey away on the Blue Mountain Express. We got on the train in the evening and later climbed into the sleeper berths. We woke up to the smiling faces of my grandparents, who met the train with flasks of hot coffee and crisp vadas (lentil doughnuts) fried right on the platform.

Unlike these short overnight journeys, the trip from Madras to Bombay was satisfyingly long. The train left Madras at dawn and reached Bombay the following morning. My brother and I had all day and all night in the train to stake out corners, play card games, make friends with the other children, run riot through the compartment, annoy ticket inspectors by singing to the rhythm of the train, and most important, partake of our neighbours' tiffin carriers.

The tiffin carrier is a simple yet wonderful Indian invention. Several cylindrical stainless-steel containers are stacked and held together with a metal fastener that serves as a handle. Although the word tiffin means light food, the tiffin carrier can hold anything. The one I took daily to school had two containers—the bottom one for a hearty rice dish and the top one for a vegetable.

If my school lunch box with its measly two containers was a Manhattan town house, the Marwari matron's tiffin carrier was the Empire State Building, with more than a dozen stainless steel containers. She opened each container at a strategic point in our journey. At dawn, we had the roti and potato saag. At 10 a.m., a snack of crisp kakda (wafers) speckled with pepper. For lunch, a bounty of stuffed parathas (flatbreads filled with mashed potatoes, spinach, radish, paneer and other such goodies).

My mother had brought lunch in a tiffin carrier, too—petal-soft idlis wrapped in banana leaves and slathered with coconut chutney. Idlis are steamed dumplings made from a rice and lentil batter that is allowed to ferment for a day. American idlis are hard and don't possess the tangy sourdough taste. To eat the authentic spongy idli in all its glory, you have to go to Madras and get invited to someone's home for breakfast.

My mother always made idlis for train travel because, among their other virtues, they keep well. The Marwari boys scooped hers up with gusto and wolfed them down with gentle, satisfied grunts.

As the sun climbed high in the sky, the train rolled into the arid plains of Andhra Pradesh. I began salivating for mangoes. The moment the train stopped at Renigunta station, passengers jumped off on an urgent errand. My father and I disdained the train-side hawkers who carried baskets of high-priced, inferior mangoes and sprinted towards the stalls on either side of the platform. About a dozen different types of mangoes were piled high: custardy Mulgoas, robust sweet-sour Alphonsos, ultra-juicy Banganapallis, parrot-beaked Bangaloras and finally, the Rasalu, the king of mangoes in terms of sweetness.

A few minutes of intense bargaining followed, fuelled by the fact that the train would leave the station at any minute. Just as the whistle blew and the guard waved his green flag, my father and I jumped back on the train carrying armloads of juicy mangoes, which tasted even better for the adrenaline and tension that had surrounded their purchase. My brother and I sat at the open door of the train as it rumbled slowly through the Deccan Plateau, slurping mangoes and waving at villagers. I threw the mango seeds into opportune clearings and imagined entire mango orchards rising behind me.

Almost every station in India sells a regional specialty that causes passengers to dart on and off trains. My parents have awakened me at 3 a.m. just to taste the hot milk at Erode station in Tamil Nadu. Anyone passing by Nagpur station is entreated to buy its glorious oranges. Allahabad, home to Hinduism and the Ganga River, is famous for its guavas; Agra, where the Taj Mahal stands, has wonderful pedas (chewy squares of candy made with milk). Simla, called queen of the hill stations by the British, was known for its apples. Kerala, where my father spent his childhood and still leaves his heart, has the best plantain fritters, fried in coconut oil on the platform.

As if the stations weren't distraction enough, a steady stream of vendors brought food on to the train as well. Our mid-afternoon card games were almost always interrupted by teenage boys in khaki shorts selling coffee. 'Kapi, kapi, kapi,' they would call, pausing to check out who had the best hand of cards. Frequently, the person with the best hand ordered a round of coffee for the group, inadvertently giving away his advantage.

If we were lucky enough to stop at Andhra Pradesh at dinnertime, my parents would buy us aromatic biryanis. Andhra cooks make the best biryanis in the world. They combine basmati rice, succulent meats marinated in a yogurt-mint sauce with ginger, garlic, green chillies and a long list of ground roasted spices. These ingredients are slow-cooked in a vessel with a lid sealed on with dough, so that the flavours don't escape. Being Brahmins and, therefore, vegetarians, my parents encouraged us to eat vegetable biryanis. The only times I almost strayed were when I encountered the mouth-watering smell of lamb biryanis on trains.

Having lived in the United States for fifteen years, I made my most recent annual visit to India a few months ago. My father considerately booked us on the Shatabdi (Century) Express from Madras to Bangalore. My parents were thrilled to be showing off the Shatabdi Express. 'It is just like your US aeroplanes,' my mother exclaimed. Indeed it was. Fully air conditioned with reclining seats, this super-fast train is frequented by business people and foreigners. It leaves on time and doesn't make random stops. The sealed windows and air conditioning keep away heat, dust and stray vendors. As soon as we got on, two plastic-gloved attendants gave us bottled water, newspapers and a hot breakfast

> Often, the best part is before you actually enter the train.

served from a trolley. In a scant four hours, we had reached Bangalore.

Now, I live in Bangalore and I use the Shatabdi and double decker trains many, many times. Often, the best part is before you actually enter the train. In fact, the railways are an institution that has successfully added technology and conveniences while retaining the culture and charisma that make it so alluring for many of us.

ABOARD THE VIVEK EXPRESS

Aasheesh Sharma

On a hot April afternoon in 1853, as the first steam locomotive pulled out of Bombay's Bori Bunder station and chugged towards Thane, train travel was born in this country. That would make the Indian Railways and me the same sun sign! This nugget of 'Kaun Banega Crorepati' meets Bejan Daruwalla trivia made me chuckle to myself. So, when, in the 160th anniversary year of the Indian Railways, an opportunity came along to ride the Vivek Express, aboard the longest single train journey in India, it was difficult to let go. What could have been a better way to experience the disparate sights, sounds, smells and people of the nation, doing close to 4,300 kilometres (more than one-tenth of the earth's circumference) in four nights and three days, than by train? The Mahatma might have agreed. Around the nation in eighty-

---

The original version of this article was published in *Brunch*, the weekly magazine of the *Hindustan Times*, on 19 May 2013, with the headline 'Such A Long Journey'.

two hours! A trip by train from one end of the country to another is special because it is microcosmic of the Indian way of life, the very idea of India. On the Vivek Express, of course, the role of the railways in uniting a multiplicity of people across diverse states permeates through strongly. The train connects Dibrugarh, India's northeastern frontier point, with Kanyakumari, the southernmost tip, traversing through Assam, West Bengal, Odisha, Andhra Pradesh, Tamil Nadu, Kerala and then Tamil Nadu again. During the journey, hauled by a diesel engine in non-electrified territory and by electric engine in the electrified zone, it crosses through a rainbow of regional railway zones: the Northeast Frontier Railway, the Eastern Railway, the South Eastern Railway, the East Coast Railway, the South Central Railway and finally, the Southern Railway. As if this wasn't compelling enough, I had my own good reasons to have developed a fondness for train travel. I grew up in a household where my English professor father took a lot of pride in being addressed as 'gypsy scholar' by his friends and colleagues. Dad, who died fighting a violent cancer in 2008, said he had left unclaimed baggage worth many thousands in the waiting rooms of the Indian Railways during some of the hundreds of journeys he undertook, criss-crossing the country, whenever wanderlust gripped him. Our dining table conversations often centred on the number of stations between Bombay and Bhusawal and all those wonderful times he had slept on a bale of cotton on a railway platform. So, I didn't have to try hard to develop a soft corner for the railways.

Boning up on railway fiction and exotic travelogues might help you prepare mentally to spend eighty-two hours on a train that cuts from its northeastern tip to its southernmost extremity. But as India flashes by the window, nothing prepares you for what lies inside: a yatra that opens your eyes to ways of living, travelling and surviving the Great Indian Railways experience. Perhaps, a line by author Paul Theroux about the romance of travel comes close: 'You go away for a long time and return a different person—you never come all the way back.'

In 1881, the British set up a sixty-five-kilometre metre gauge line from Dibrugarh in north Assam to

But as India flashes by the window, nothing prepares you for what lies inside: a yatra that opens your eyes to ways of living, travelling and surviving the Great Indian Railways experience.

the Margherita Garden Estate, mainly for transportation of tea and coal. Today, Dibrugarh, a bustling town on the Himalayan foothills, is one of the two cities in the country, which is not a state capital, to have Rajdhani Express originating from it (the other being Bilaspur in Chhattisgarh). On this trip, photographer Arijit Sen and I flew to Dibrugarh on a sultry May afternoon. The skies opened up as soon as we landed in Assam. 'A good omen!' exclaimed Arijit. After braving a downpour, as we waited for the stationmaster and train staff at the crew lobby, we chanced upon an intriguing procedure: driver Mohammad Rahimuddin (fifty-five), blowing hard into an alcometer for a breathalyser test done to ensure drivers aren't tipsy when they guide the train. That done, he got an update on the locomotive's load capacity, electrical output and power certification from the staff before he headed to the pilot's cabin. 'Most of the twenty-two coaches of the Vivek Express have been built in the integrated rail coach factory at Kapurthala and the rest at Perambur. A majority of passengers on the train are soldiers manning our borders since China is just 220 kilometres from Dibrugarh,' the amiable station in-charge, R. Bhattacharjee, told us over teabag chai and biscuits.

The Vivek Express runs on a weekly frequency. It starts every Saturday from Dibrugarh and the return journey takes place next

Saturday from Kanyakumari. It takes you across more than 600 stations, halting at fifty-six major destinations spread across eight states in two-tier air-conditioned comfort for just ₹3,475. The ticket for third A/C is ₹2,305, the sleeper class ₹925 and for the general class ₹545.

As I settle my portly eighty-five-kg frame into the lower berth, an old Indian Railways tagline: 'To learn a thousand dialects, eat a thousand cuisines and meet a million people, you need just one berth', comes to mind. 'That's because you are riding on one of the world's largest rail networks, touching more than 10,000 destinations across India. The Indian Railways runs 12,000 trains every day across 64,460 kilometres stopping at 7,133 stations. It employs around 13.4 lakh employees and serves fifty-two lakh meals every day,' goes the pitch. When one negotiates more than 4,000 kilometres on the longest train journey in India, one comes across mountains, rivers, backwaters and the sea. One unravels local tongues and makes friends with fellow passengers even as one's taste buds explode with a smattering of food flavours. Food, yes, as usual, it manages to derail my train of thought! I make my way across my two-tier A/C through the vestibule and decide to explore the train.

In the three-tier A/C section, as Boney M's 'Hooray, hooray, it's a holi-holiday/ What a world of fun for everyone, holi-holiday' blares from their smartphones, two nattily dressed Naga girls from Dimapur stands out with their exuberant disposition. 'I am like, super-excited!' announces Avi Chishi, a twenty-four-year-old student of theology, as she turns the speakers off and gives her headphones to her friend, Vikali Sumi, twenty-two. 'We hadn't ever ventured beyond Guwahati till yesterday. And today, here we are, headed to the tip of the subcontinent on a trip of a lifetime,' says Sumi. 'Inside the campus of Dimapur's New Life Bible College, we mostly listen to gospel musicians such as Paul Baloche and Max

Locado. But on a holiday, we can choose to listen to classic rock,' adds Sumi. A few coaches down, a few of their friends from Bible College are having an animated discussion on technology and its many-fangled temptations. Even the religious-minded could find some good use for a Net nanny, it appears.

As the hilly terrain of Assam makes way for Bengal, rows and rows of thatched roofed houses run alongside the rail track. The landscape becomes flatter and on the garishly painted walls of the rare concrete dwelling, advertisements for Amul Macho *'yeh to bada toing hai'* innerwear and Ultratech cement compete with Bengali slogans of railway employee unions.

'Doi, doi, mishti doi.' At Durgapur, the first vendors of sweetened curd bring that unmistakable Bengali touch to the platform. With a thirty-minute stop for refuelling and change of engine from diesel to electric, the halt is ideal to make one's acquaintance with the charioteers of our train, one thinks. So, between the industrial town best known for its steel plant and Asansol, we request loco pilot, R.B. Ram, and his assistant, Rajiv Kumar, to allow us a peek into their cabin and they oblige. Outside the drivers' cabin, truck after truck of coal extracted from the Raniganj coalfields just outside Durgapur drive past. The undulating landscape is a maze of giant factories, tin sheds, lorry drivers and electrical wires. Inside, with the assurance of a pro, Ram is shouting instructions to his junior on impending railway signals. Manning their console, with meters to check air flow, braking pressure and speed, needs knowledge of both the mechanical and electrical aspects of locomotive engineering, says Ram (fifty-three), a native of Mughalsarai in Uttar Pradesh, who has made Asansol his home for the twenty years he has been with the railways.

Kumar is just one of the faces of the indefatigable, nameless Vivek Express staff who ensure that this lifeline for thousands of people in the Northeast and southern India reaches its destination on time, again and again. The men behind the machine include the ticket inspectors, the drivers and the guards who change after every 250 kilometres. So, on an average, for the 4,273-kilometre long journey, you get a changeover close to eighteen times. On the morning of the third day, we approach Andhra Pradesh's Vijayawada junction, one of the busiest stations in southern India, which handles more than 320 trains every day. Soon there are vendors selling piping fresh dosai, idlis and vadais.

Being confined for hours together in a common space brings even the most introverted characters out of their shell and spontaneous friendships formed on trains are sometimes known to last lifetimes. Shyamoshree (thirty-four), a homemaker from Dimapur, Nagaland, for instance, is travelling with her five-year-old daughter, Ashtha, to Kottayam to visit family friends. They met Ratna Ghosh and her six-year-old daughter, Sayantika, natives of Dibrugarh, a few hours back on the train and have become great friends since. The two girls play antakshri, Atlas, watch games on Shyamoshree's laptop and transform themselves into announcers on the train's non-existent public address system every time it slows down at a station.

As one takes leave of Andhra Pradesh towards Tamil Nadu, one notices a group of travellers preparing to de-board at Katpadi Junction, near the Christian Medical College (CMC), Vellore. Swarup Dutta, a thirty-two-year-old telecom engineer from Dibrugarh, is taking his father Subir Kumar Dutta (sixty), a former National Assurance Company executive, for treatment of his lower back. 'The extent of personal care for patients there is much better than Assam. So one doesn't mind the travel,' says Dutta Junior. Arati Sarkar (fifty-nine), a housewife from Assam, who is travelling with her daughter and granddaughter to CMC to get a gum infection treated, agrees. 'It's a shame that the Northeast which is home to 40 million people, almost equal to the population of England, doesn't have decent medical facilities,' says Sarkar.

At Chengannur, the Vivek Express turns into a ghost train. Most of the migrant workers have alighted. The general, sleeper and air-conditioned coaches are deserted and one does a recce to find out if there are any travellers left. It is here, in the two-tier compartment, that the smiling countenance and sparkling eyes of Sister Janet Baby catch your attention. Almost hidden on a side-berth, the thirty-seven-year-old assistant teacher in Arunachal Pradesh's Miao diocese, is viewing the lush green landscape from the window, as she prepares to reach home to her village in Thiruvananthapuram district. 'This has been my first trip on this train and it was special. The last time we came by plane spending a steep ₹20,000, I could never mingle with other sisters and fathers. From eating together, to recounting stories, to moving around and meeting other sisters on the Vijayawada platform, it can only be possible here. That is the biggest charm of a train journey,' she says. On the fourth morning, in the final stretch of our sojourn after Thiruvananthapuram Central, through cajolement and coercion, we persuade Senior Guard M. Abubacker (fifty-seven), to let us travel with him in the brake-van. It turns out to be the best part of our eighty-two-hour journey. We are cruising through the backwaters, with the landscape a lush expanse of green, with swaying palms, the smell of the ocean nearby and the company of a born storyteller. We count four tunnels and three trains pass us by, as Abubacker Sahib opens his trunk (that has among other sundry supplies such as flags, maps, torches and rulebooks, a detonator) and heart to us. The guard's cabin is a hallowed space. Unlike engine drivers (two of them confined to a small space), he is the lord of all he surveys. 'Sir, I am like a one-man army. I don't need assistants,' says Abubacker as he goes on to explain how a guard may need to put a detonator on the tracks in case of a derailment to protect the train. When he joined the railways thirty-four years ago, the native of Alleppey, known for its powder beaches and backwaters, Abubacker served as a forge-man. He cleared an exam to become a guard and now, after marrying off both his daughters to 'suitable' boys in the Gulf (where else!), he has no unfinished personal agendas. Abubacker's sense of pride comes from a sense of finality, 'After close to twelve guards have changed hands over 4,200 kilometres, in the last stretch, for the final eighty-odd kilometres from Thiruvananthapuram to Kanyakumari, a guard from Quilon division is guiding the Vivek Express, the longest train journey in the country. Personally, it is a matter of great honour, sir!' The pride is infectious. Suddenly, even my photographer colleague and I are gripped by a sense of having achieved something substantial. After Chengannur, with the train deserted, I perch myself on the top berth and lie back, thinking about the import and magnitude of where we've come so far. We've been travelling for more than eighty hours! Of the 600 stations that fell en route to Kanyakumari, the train halted at fifty-six.

Beyond the statistics, as I look back at the journey, a smile forms on my face remembering the ensemble cast of characters I befriended on this unifying odyssey of a journey, thanks to the Vivek Express: a soldier longing to be back home on annual leave, a son taking his father for treatment to Vellore, two teenagers high on life and freedom getting their taste of unexplored terrain for the first time outside the Northeast, a sibling who is taking care of his paralysed elder brother, nuns who spread love and peace on both sides of the train and the daughter of mixed parentage who's as comfortable speaking in Tamil as she is in Nagamese. One by one, most of my co-passengers de-board the train and promise to keep in touch and meet again. The context might be different, but my mind wanders back to author Khushwant Singh's novel *Delhi*, where his protagonist, an ageing guide, quotes these lines from the Mahabharata: 'As two pieces of wood floating on the ocean come together at one time and are again separated, even such is the union of living creatures in this world.' On the fifth morning, at Kanyakumari, the final station, a few stragglers alight from the train, apart from the train staff. Beyond that is the sea. Kanyakumari, at the Cape Comorin, is the Land's End of the country and believed to have multicoloured sands. It is at the tip of India where the Indian Ocean and the Arabian Sea meet the Bay of Bengal. It is, perhaps, one of the few stations in the world with a sunrise observation roof and sunset and sunrise times posted on an information booth. The sleepy township is revered for its Kanyakumari shrine and the Vivekananda Memorial, named after the Bengali philosopher, which becomes an island at high tide. The legend goes that standing in the waters of Kanyakumari, if one had three legs, one could plant them each in the Bay of Bengal, the Indian Ocean and the Arabian Sea. It is a logical conclusion for a journey where all Indian rivers of faith, creed, culture and languages finally submerge. The track stops here.

CHANGING LANES

Kartik Iyengar
Contribution: Jonas Olsson & Devyani Kalvit

It happened to me ten years ago on a busy Friday afternoon. A million vehicles seemed to have suddenly descended in front of my taxi. It seemed as if there was a conspiracy to get me stuck in a traffic jam for hours and make me miss my flight to Bangalore.

The incessant honking was driving me crazy as Manjunath, my cab driver, tried to navigate recklessly through the chaotic traffic.

I muttered a few expletives under my breath as I asked in anticipation, 'Will we get to the airport in time for my flight, Manjunath?' Pat came the reply, 'Sorry, Sahib, Not possible. Take the train instead. We are very close to the station now. Should I?'

I could sense the reflection of my irritation in his curt reply.

I had three important appointments lined up in the evening: a job interview, an uncomfortable date with my fiancé and a meeting that would decide the fate of my writing career.

My life inched at a snail's pace between manually operated traffic signals and unruly traffic.

'Quick! Tell me, Sahib? Do you want to take the train instead? It leaves in thirty minutes,' said Manjunath impatiently. He was an irritable man who claimed to be thirty but looked sixty years old. Perhaps, his reckless driving skills and foul temper had made him age prematurely.

'Fine, I'll take the train. Take me to the station, but drive slowly. You drive like a maniac! Have to get to Bangalore at any cost,' I said. Once I decided to take the train, I had to make phone calls to explain the reason for my absence that evening and request moving my three appointments to tomorrow.

He recklessly jumped a signal and took an abrupt turn towards the railway station. My stomach was in my mouth when I glanced at my watch. There wasn't much time left. A short, bumpy ride and a few hapless pedestrians later, Manjunath brought his relic of a taxi to a screeching halt right in front of the ticket counter.

'There! Run, Sahib! You have twenty minutes!' said Manjunath. I thrust a couple of hundred-rupee notes at him. He seemed unhappy. I think he wanted more for all his unwanted advice and for giving me a second lease of life after the hell-ride. A train journey seemed a lot safer option than prolonged exposure to Manjunath, so I added a fifty-rupee note to the deal.

I needed to calm down. I stood in a short queue and managed to get a seat in a general coach. Maybe my luck was changing? However, I was pleasantly surprised by the efficiency of the ticketing process. The lady at the counter thrust out a ticket with the dexterity of a psychopath skillfully flashing a knife about to seal my fate.

I had to get to Platform Number 4, which was at the other end of the station. One had to take a flight of stairs towards the platform. The near-empty foot overbridge close by was surprisingly clean and empty.

When I reached the centre of the bridge, I paused briefly to glance at the railway tracks below. There was a breathtaking view of the setting sun. It had the much needed calming effect on me. The gentle breeze wafted across the bridge. It seemed to augur the start of something good.

I hadn't in my wildest dreams imagined myself feeling comfortable and relaxed at a railway station. One by one, my elitist beliefs about train journeys and railway stations were being shattered.

The small station had four platforms and was dotted with trees along the sides; a large water tank towering over the trees; the endless railway tracks ran parallel, joined at times by curved tracks merging beautifully.

I looked on silently as the setting sun cast its golden rays on Platform Number 4. It was a small, clean platform that was about a kilometre long. I glanced across the four platforms from my vantage point and realized that there were no more than fifty people at the railway station across the platforms.

I could hear the silence of the evening being gently underlined by the muffled chugs of an approaching train from far away. The sweet smell of summer drifted across the bridge and brought back childhood memories and a gentle sense of calm.

As I lazily walked towards the platform, the breeze seemed to whisper something in my ear. I suppose it wanted to tell me to take it easy and let the glory of the present smash my condescending attitude that somehow comes with the years once you grow up.

I descended the flight of stairs towards the platform. I was now looking forward to the train journey. The short walk across the bridge over the railway tracks seemed to have sucked out the horrors inflicted upon me by the terrible taxi ride.

It was symbolic. The taxi was the perfect embodiment of the mad rush in our everyday lives. The flight over bridge was the healer. The endless railway tracks had many lessons to teach. But now, I was ready to unlearn what I already knew.

I had no luggage, except a small rucksack that packed my

notebook, an iPod and my laptop together. I found the spot where my compartment would halt with much ease. Everything was contrary to the way I had expected it to be so far.

I would get on a train after many years. I leisurely walked across the sleepy platform. I spotted a calm man in uniform. I presumed he must be the stationmaster. He had attained nirvana simply by looking at trains come and go by.

A small shed, that was his office, sported a large black board on which the train schedules had been handwritten using a wet chalk. The tea stall by the side brought in a sea of memories. I used to travel by train with my parents.

My father would take me across to the tea stall, and it was a moment of huge excitement for me. Parle glucose biscuits, plastic bags of delicious chips and simmering hot tea, were some of the goodies that I would make him buy for me while we waited for our train.

While we would wait, other trains would come and go. The mad rush when the train arrived would nourish my soul and the sense of emptiness on the platform once it left would leave a sense of yearning in me.

My father once told me that it reminds him of the sea. One can watch the waves rush in and gently kiss the shore and then quickly recede. You just stand there as a mute spectator as your cup of life fills up to the brim and empties out. He said that the experience enriches you as a person.

> My father once told me that a railway station reminds him of the sea. One can watch the waves rush in and gently kiss the shore and then quickly recede.

Cup of tea in hand, I tipped the stall owner a full rupee for a cup of chai that cost five-rupees and walked away. The tea stall owner seemed to take no notice of my generous tip. Probably, inflation had corroded the roots of small tea stalls as well. A mere 20 per cent tip seemed to have failed to evoke a response.

I stood sipping the ambrosial tea and watched a little boy trying to help his mother near the water taps. She patiently accommodated his plea for help, as he excitedly held a clay pot with his small hands, and smiled and kept the tap running for longer than necessary.

More water spilled outside than flowing into it as the small hands struggled to hold on to the heavy pot. There was no sense of hurry in her to get the job done.

An old man slept on the floor, oblivious to the surroundings. He snored gently as the slanting rays of the setting sun warmed his back. It was a snooze a busy, rich man could only wish for. No sleeping pills would ever buy him this kind of a sleep.

I lumbered across to an idyllic peepal tree beside the tea stall. It had a circular cemented platform to sit on. The wind rustled the leaves and the earthy aroma gave me a sense of peace. I looked yonder to spot two men, sitting on a bench, in the adjacent platform having a highly animated conversation.

Watching them from a distance, I could sense it was an engaging discussion. Maybe, there was a reason why they chose to have a conversation here instead of a grand coffee shop. They surely didn't look like they were waiting for a train anyway.

I looked around to spot a stray mongrel wag its tail in front of a mendicant sitting near the flight of stairs that led to the foot overbridge. He had a small aluminum bowl in front of him that he held out to every passer-by with his fingerless hands. He had no legs either. Life is unfair, I thought to myself.

A coolie clad in the classic red kurta, white dhoti and golden badge with the number '786' strapped on the arm, stopped and asked me if I needed help with my luggage. I said no and pointed to my rucksack. His face fell and he walked away. I couldn't help but smile when a fleeting thought about the lack of dignity of labour in the corporate sector crossed my mind then.

The wind gently caressed my hair as I looked around to see a train chugging in from afar. The lady on the loudspeaker was making an announcement in different languages. It was my train to Bangalore.

The child in me had woken up as I watched the train chug in closer. By now, I was wildly excited about my first train journey in years.

A hawker selling peanuts, in neatly folded paper cones, walked briskly towards the edge of the platform where I stood.

The decibel level around me increased as the train majestically chugged in. The sleepy platform had suddenly come alive. Oblivious to the people around me, I watched in awe as the engine made a loud entrance. The compartments passed by slowly in front of me.

Chai! Garam Chai! chanted a loud voice right beside me as he jostled with other passengers and hawkers who now flocked on the platform as the train chugged closer. Suddenly, I was lost in a crowd.

I watched in awe as all thoughts about getting to Bangalore in time for my three appointments took a backseat. All that mattered now was the train journey. I patiently watched the impatient ones scramble ahead at the sight of the train as it halted. Very few people chose to get off but many tried to board the train at the same time, clumsily managing their belongings.

I suppressed a smile as I watched with glee the sheer pleasure of finally being the last one to board. Unlike my track record of being the last one to board an aircraft and having my name called out. It made me feel human.

Once I boarded, I walked into my six-berth coupe. My fellow passengers included an old man in his seventies who sat beside me. He wore a neatly ironed white kurta-pyjama and comfortable-looking brown floaters. A young girl in her late teens in blue jeans and a blue sweatshirt and sneakers sat on the opposite window seat.

A plump middle-aged woman dressed in a pink sari with floral prints and a matching blouse sat with packets of food between her and the girl. A newly married couple gazed longingly at each other, lost in a make-believe world of their own. The mehndi on the woman's palms and the sheer number of glass bangles on her wrists were testimonial of their recent wedding.

The two side-berths remained vacant.

I had expected the compartment to be overcrowded, full of smelly, sweaty people, and here was another myth busted. The train was now moving as the announcements of departure could be heard on the loudspeakers.

Exchanging pleasantries with my fellow passengers, I shoved my rucksack under the lower berth where I sat by the window, lest it bother my co-passengers. Within ten minutes, the train had picked up speed and we were on our way.

My fellow passengers who had been complete strangers to one another had by now started chatting as though they were childhood friends and knew each other forever.

It was close to 7.30 p.m. when I remembered that I had to make phone calls to change my appointments. 'Excuse me, I need to make a few calls, I'll be right back,' I said as I clutched my cell phone and stood up.

'Beta, forget it. You won't get the signal. Even if you do, the signal will be bad in this sector. I know it. Better to message them and enjoy the journey,' said the old man.

I looked at my phone and felt sick. The signal was very weak. I tried making calls and they just wouldn't go through. I should have made the calls from the railway station itself.

'They were very important calls and now I'm finished!' I said as I slumped back into my seat. I was disappointed.

The young girl giggled and pretended to look outside the window. The woman smiled and caressed her food packets as though they were her pets. The old man folded his arms and couldn't stop grinning. The newly-wed couple didn't care.

There was complete silence for about a couple of minutes. I took in the gentle sounds of the whirring fans and the rhythmic rounds of the moving train. I wasn't just shaking because of a moving train, but was shaking like a leaf from within when I thought about the three missed opportunities of my life.

'People these days, always in a hurry, aren't they, Madam?' said the old man to the plump woman, who was busy arranging the neatly packed packets of warm food on the seat. I chose to ignore the obvious remark.

'It's the age of the phones and Internet, Sir, they do not know how to enjoy the joys of travel,' she said as she gingerly went about arranging a newspaper as a tablecloth. Then, looking at me she said, 'You'll be all right in a bit. Why don't you switch off your cell phone and relax a bit, Beta?'

I stared at my cell phone for some time and nodded meekly. She was right.

Anyway, nothing had gone according to plan for me that day. I chose to listen to her and go with the flow, and take in the present moments instead. There was nothing left for me to lose.

'Tell us about your phone calls, Mister? Why are they so important? And what do you do for a living?' asked the impish girl with a smile. I was taken aback by her brazen intrusion of my privacy.

Since I had decided to play along, I told everybody that I was a writer by choice, badly in need of a job. It seemed like a dream now. I told them about being in a troubled relationship where I just didn't know what to do.

They heard me out patiently when I told them that I would be missing out on my big break to co-author a management book with a renowned Rhodes Scholar about the strategies of running large businesses.

I really didn't know if they understood my troubles or empathized with me and I couldn't care less. They were considerate enough not to judge or be more inquisitive. The sweet couple heard me initially, got bored and went back to their dreamy world and chose to ignore my rants.

'Here, Beta, please have something to eat?' said the pleasant woman as she handed me paper plate full of rich, oily food, 'Trust me, you'll know exactly what to do when you meet her next.'

I smiled at her and graciously accepted–not just the food, but her verdict as well.

Essentially, it was up to me to decide whether I wanted to continue my troubled relationship with my fiancé, with whom I had once embarked upon a journey when the going was good.

I looked around at my fellow passengers who were busy sharing jokes and dinner, and dragged myself into the conversation and asked the girl, 'So, tell me, what do you think of train journeys?'

In between nibbles and giggles she replied, 'Look, Mister, unlike airplanes or flying coffins where one cannot open windows and let the wind ruffle your hair, train journeys are different. What's the point?' said the girl, giggling and laughing at her own joke. She had a point.

Out of the blue, the young bride looked at me and finally spoke, 'Mister, even if it meant looking out of the window and watching the world go by at a steady pace, what can you see from an airplane window ever?'

'True! Where is the romance?' asked the true-to-goodness loyal mate. 'We couldn't get an air-conditioned compartment, but we still chose to go for our honeymoon by train so we can spend more time at an easy pace.'

They did make sense. I felt happy in a strange way that I had missed my flight, taken a train and was now incommunicado.

The old man helped himself to another large helping and

said, 'Just so you know, Son, from my experience I can tell you this much. If your prospective employer cannot wait for you just because you missed a flight, don't take up the job. It will kill you. The trick for a long life is the pace with which you live it...'

The plump woman nodded in agreement and the couple briefly looked at the wise one as he let loose this pearl of wisdom. He made sense to me then. It would make me think.

A brief silence followed. There were no reactions. Topics changed quickly. Their talks and laughter continued, I gazed out of the window and saw distant lights flicker and disappear into the darkness of the night. I wondered if the disappearing lights were an indication of things to come?

Absence and an unreachable cell phone could be disastrous for many busy bees. Would my prospective employer look upon my absence as a sign of unprofessionalism and strike me off?

Would my fiancé misconstrue my disappearance as a sign of my walking out of our troubled relationship? Would the Rhodes Scholar choose some other writer?

As these thoughts plagued me, the chugging of the fast moving train and the gentle breeze on my face lifted my spirits. Much as I tried to worry or try to delve into depths of panic and depression, I just couldn't.

Instead, I was being pulled into a different world. A world of simple, light-hearted banter where strangers become friends for a journey and wouldn't drag it on unless they chose to continue once the train reached its destination.

The pace of the journey where the environment lends itself to make one think and reflect unlike other modes of transportation; this I realized is what defines train travel.

Close to 10 p.m., as I took my rucksack and climbed to the upper berth, I stared at the small, rectangular steel plate just above the berth. Number '13' was etched on it.

Wasn't this number supposed to be unlucky? Fluffing up my rucksack to use as a pillow, I settled in and started playing with my iPod. I didn't find anything interesting to listen to that night since I couldn't get any sleep.

The old man and the plump woman had dozed off in the lower berths. The girl had taken the upper berth, adjacent to mine. Huddled under a blanket, she was staring at the roof. She was wide-awake and lost in thought.

The pace of the journey where the environment lends itself to make one think and reflect unlike other modes of transportation; this I realized is what defines train travel.

'Mister, may I say something if you don't mind?' said the young girl.

'Sure, shoot. Anyway, my day couldn't get more awesome,' I said, not looking away from my iPod.

'Look, I wonder why you need to meet that Rhodes Scholar at all to write your book. It's about large business conglomerates, isn't it?'

I nodded, toying with my iPod.

'Are you even aware that you are travelling right now on the world's second largest rail network under one single management? Do you know that it's the largest network in Asia? Do you even have an idea of the opportunity that life's just given to you today?' she said excitedly.

It was obvious she wasn't getting any sleep either. The train was moving at a fast pace and the gentle rocking was making me think. I didn't respond.

Not that it mattered much to me as she continued to speak, 'Folks like you talk about Corporate Social Responsibility at all B-Schools. Of the twenty-three million passengers who use Indian Railways everyday, the majority are unreserved passengers.

Something you might want to bear in mind when you look for your new job. Right?'

She had a point. Though I wasn't looking at her, she knew she had my full attention.

'If I were to tell you that the total distance covered by these 14,300 trains everyday equals three and a half times the distance to the moon, would you please write the book yourself? I could help you if you wish…for someday even I want to be a writer like you…' she said with a faraway look in her eyes. 'OK, goodnight!'

'Goodnight,' I said and turned and looked at her. She was now lost in a world of her own again.

She was a smart cookie who'd just helped me find an answer to my third challenge. Not just that, she had given me more ideas.

Looking back, I got my inspiration from fellow passengers that evening. Today, I am a successful management consultant in my own right. I have written many books and published many papers on strategy since then.

The girl, who gave me the advice on not having my work co-authored, now co-authors most of my books. In fact, all my published works are co-authored, either by her or by other youngsters like her, who respect assets like the Indian Railways that have always existed in our great nation.

The old man I met on the train became my mentor on corporate matters. It turned out that he had successfully incubated many technology startups in India and abroad. He passed away last week.

I also discovered that the plump lady was a chartered accountant who became a homemaker. It took me a lot of persuasion to make her manage my tax matters.

The meeting with my fiancé never happened. She refused to meet me after I stood her up.

Berth Number 13 changed my life forever. I changed lanes that night.

KANGRA: THE LAND OF THE WHITE MOUNTAIN

Premola Ghose

The lush, well-watered valley of Kangra lies between the Siwaliks and the Dhauladhar mountains of the Outer Himalaya. Known as Dev Bhumi, it is indeed a valley of the gods, rich in religious sites and an Arcadian landscape that is now threatened by affluence and development. What best way to see the valley than by train! The train provides intimate glimpses of the countryside as it weaves its way up the mountain, through fields and villages. One can even glimpse the interiors of homes, and sometimes butterflies are allowed to hitch a ride! And, there are always rewarding encounters with the people of Kangra!

It was on one of my many journeys by car, from Pathankot to Kangra, that I first encountered the blue and beige Kangra Valley Railway (KVR). Like a running thread, the train crisscrossed the road we were travelling along as we moved into the heart of this valley. The KVR is a small metre gauge track running from Pathankot in the Punjab plains to Joginder Nagar in the Mandi district of Himachal Pradesh. It takes more than eight hours to cover a distance of 164 kilometres. There are no sharp curves as the gradient is not steep. In fact, as P S A Berridge wrote in *Couplings to the Khyber* (1929): 'The line, keeping the 16,000 ft snowcapped peaks in view nearly all the way, runs through smallholdings, terraced fields of rice, vegetables and fruit, separated by hedges of cacti, clumps of bamboo, spear grass, which in the higher parts give way to pines and firs and deodar trees.'

In 1849, Dr Jameson, Superintendent of the Botanical Gardens of the Northwest Provinces, introduced the tea plant in the Kangra Valley and soon tea plantations run by the British extended through Palampur, Dharamsala and Baijnath. Tea brought the development of colonial towns with the army, hospitals, churches and schools. However, travel to Kangra from the plains was not easy and several recommendations were made to build a railway line to improve communications to these remote regions. As early as 1902, there was a suggestion for an alternate route to Dalhousie as road travel there was difficult especially for the movement of troops. Initially, the plan was to build a railway line from Pathankot to Nurpur (26 kilometres), and in 1912 the Railway Board sanctioned this. In 1914, the extension of this line to Baijnath was also cleared. However since the traffic was limited, another scheme was proposed—aerial ropeways from Nagrota West to Kangra; Kangra to Dharamsala; and Kangra to Palampur. The First World War, however, took its toll on men and finances and the whole idea was shelved.

Finally, it was the proposal for a hydroelectric power plant at Joginder Nagar that led to the creation of this railway track to carry heavy machinery. Work on this railway began in 1925-26 and the 'first sod' was laid by the Governor of Punjab. The line was opened to goods traffic in 1928 and to general traffic by 1929. The KVR was financed by the governments of India and Punjab and was the best-aligned railways of its time, indeed it was considered to be a masterpiece. Since the railway finances were separated from the general budget, it was possible to start work without much delay. However, the expenditure exceeded the budget and led to much criticism at that time.

Unlike the Kalka-Shimla Railway, this was not a sahib's train, taking the Raj to cooler climes, equipped with leather seats and polished brass fitments and the chhota-hazari stops serving colonial repasts. Instead, it was a plebian train to take raw materials and labour to Joginder Nagar, where Uhl Hydro Project was being constructed to provide electricity to undivided Punjab and Delhi. The train has continued to be a local train, catering to the travel needs of the people of Kangra as they go to meet relatives or shop at Palampur, and the ticket prices are much cheaper than the bus!

> Unlike the Kalka-Shimla Railway, this was not a sahib's train, taking the Raj to cooler climes, equipped with leather seats and polished brass fitments and the chhota-hazari stops serving colonial repasts

The KVR is an excellent example of how railway engineers worked in harmony with nature and their work that was sensitively conceived and carried out is indeed a tribute to the beauty of this sub-Himalayan region. Instead of using tunnelling thorough the mountains, they imaginatively worked their way around them, following the ancient routes that meandered up the valley. It is interesting to note that the KVR is the longest hill train covering more than 100 kilometres. It opened up transportation in these hills, since it was largely a passenger train. Today, the KVR still maintains the original features of the old railway line, the locomotives and rolling stock and the signal system.

H.S. Stark of the North Western Railway (NWR) wrote

glowingly about this:

'The Kangra Valley Railway proves that the railway construction engineer can create a work which is by no means out of harmony with the beauty and stateliness of the surroundings in which his allotted task has lain. Without destroying the beauty and grandeur of mountain and vale, he has revealed to the traveller a veritable land of enchantment. The line itself is where a poet and an artist would have placed it. The graceful curves of the rails, the neatness of the culverts, the symmetrical design of the bridges, the directness of the cuttings—all these are a harmonious foil to what the mighty forces of nature have moulded... A different alignment, a different mode of taking the railway through the maze of hills and valleys would have spoiled that picture—as it has so largely done in the case of the route to Simla, where the traveller spends half his time burrowing through the bowels of the earth with the scenic grandeur of the Himalayas bottled out of his vision and the hillsides made to resemble rabbit warrens.'

▪

One leaves the main bustling station of Pathankot for Platform 4, the smaller KVR station. The sound of hooting engines and staccato announcements in three languages—Punjabi, Hindi and English—blast one's ears as trains arrive from and leave for Jammu or Udhampur, which is almost the end of the line.

The blue and beige train is waiting for us on the platform and our travelling companions were locals from Kangra, soldiers and saffron-clad sadhus. It was pleasantly surprising to find small yet clean compartments fitted comfortably with fans and miniscule closet bathrooms. The atmosphere was friendly as several passengers were happy to chatter. The older passengers find it convenient, even for short journeys, as the ticket costs are low and 'what a relief' they sigh, 'there are bathrooms!'

It is from Pathankot that the traveller embarks on his journey to Joginder Nagar. Varying geographical zones unfold as the train crosses the Chakki river and the first part is through a flattish landscape, until there are views of the sprawling fort of Nurpur perched on a hilltop. Once called Dhameri, Raja Jagat Singh changed its name to Nurpur 'city of light' in the 17th century in honour of his imperial Mughal patron, Nuruddin Jahangir. The town and bazaars that lie along the gradient of the hill are a dramatic sight even today, despite the unplanned development that is turning such towns into glorified slums.

As the train meanders inland, several historic sites lie along the way, for example the rock-cut temples of Masrur at Nagrota Surian that are believed to be the inspiration for Angkor Vat in Cambodia. Built in the 8th century with traces of exquisite carving, the main temple is that of Rama, Lakshman and Sita , but the overarching presence of Shiva confirms that it was dedicated to Mahadeva.

Pong, one of the largest wetlands in north India, is another place worth visiting for its varied birdlife, including the thousands of Asian waterfowl who arrive from Central Asia, Siberia and Tibet in winter. At the next stop, Talara, the alignment of the railway lines had to be changed in 1973, when the Pong Dam was constructed on the Beas river and the portion from Jawanwala Shahr and Guler was submerged. Three years later it reopened. From here, the rocky landscape gives way to the typical rural Kangra panorama of lush rice fields and slate roofed houses and the newly aligned stretch passes through magnificent countryside with the Pong wetlands on one side and the mountains on the other.

Guler is a dusty station, situated at the end of a road, with a few desultory tea shops. It lies a little away from the village, once the home of Pandit Seu and his sons, the great Nainsukh—who emigrated to Jammu—and Manaku, under whom the Guler school of miniature paintings reached great heights. Guler was once a thriving place, known for its musicians, dancers and painters, the latter took refuge here in the 18th century following the invasion of Nadir Shah. Today, the village is a charming, prosperous place, with fertile lands supporting vegetables and fruit.

Moving east from Guler is the Banganga Gorge where one crosses one of the highlights of the line, the famous Banganga Bridge. Constructed in 1927, this bridge suffered terrible setbacks with two flash floods in quick succession.

The NWR Report records: 'Then suddenly came a 22-foot flood which made the temporary centre pier lean forward by several feet, and the engineers thought that their bridge would be swept away. The main girder was dismantled and hauled to one side, clear of the water, and the loose machinery on the banks of the nullah were strung together by cables to prevent them from being washed away by fierce current. Scarcely had the first flood subsided, when three weeks later very heavy rainfall on the foothills and in the valley brought down another and yet greater spate, filling the gorge with a 40-foot flood sweeping through the narrow cleft at a speed of twenty-five miles an hour.'

Luckily the 250-foot girder was saved from being swept away by a single mooring chain!.

From here the train climbs to Jwala Road station, the station for the two sacred Devi shrines—Jwalamukhi and Chintpurni. Jwalamukhi is one of the fifty-one Saktipithas where the goddess' tongue fell. The sanctum sanctorum is only a central pit where burns the flame and nine attendant flames. This flaming fissure is the flaming mouth of the goddess, Jwalamukhi. Chintapurni, in Una district, is also one of the Saktipithas where the charred feet of the goddess fell.

The journey from Jwalamukhi to Kangra has its dramatic moments as the train traverses two tunnels—the 25-foot-long

Dhundni and the 1,075-foot-long Daulatpur—that cut through the heart of the mountain. During the construction of the Dhundni tunnel, a heavy downpour led to the toppling of a boulder, weighing 500 tonnes—that broke into two. One part fell on the pilgrim road, and the other on the railway line! Both routes, from Jwalamukhi to Kangra, were blocked.

As the train emerges into the sunlight after the darkness of the tunnels, one is awed by the picture perfect landscape and here, the train crosses an impressive bridge and comes face to face with the mighty walls of Kangra fort, situated at the confluence of the Manjhi and Banganga rivers. Indeed we are in the heartland of the valley. The Katoch kingdom of Kangra was a prosperous one and despite the vicissitudes of history, the kings continued to rule undisturbed. Jahangir annexed the territory in 1620 and appointed a Mughal governor. Legend has it that Jahangir and Nur Jahan were fascinated by the beauty and cool climate of Kangra and planned to build a summer palace here, but fortunately, the Mughals discovered Kashmir instead!

Kangra Fort is well worth a trek just to see its haunting ruins and the dramatic landscape beyond, and also the old town of Kangra with its narrow alleys lined with shops selling religious bric-a-brac. Known as Nagarkot, it was renowned for the temple of Vajreshwari Devi, another Shaktipitha, said to be the site where the goddess' breast fell. The temple was destroyed during the 1905 earthquake and rebuilt in 1920.

En route is Reond Nullah, above which is the spectacular Steel Arch Bridge, built over a chasm whose vertical sides rise 200 feet above the river. Built by Braithwaite and Co, this 260-foot metal arched bridge, weighing 230 tonnes, was India's first steel bridge. The steelwork was initially laid out in Bombay with careful measurements, taking into account the temperature at the time its assemblage in Kangra, so that the two halves of the bridge could be brought together with great accuracy. It took six weeks to complete on-site, indeed a record achievement for such a hazardous task. An ingenious method was used—that of laying a cotton rope net beneath the bridge and above the chasm—to protect the workers from falling while they bolted sections of the bridge together. Nevertheless, they were terrorized by a man-eating leopard and hordes of monkeys!

During the years 1941-42, Europe required rails for the Second World War and since it was impossible to get anything out of Britain, the section from Nagrota to Joginder Nagar was dismantled and sent for war relief. Twelve years later the rails were refitted and this section was opened by Lal Bahadur Shastri in 1954 when he was Minister of Railways.

Kangra or Nagrota stations are the stops from where one can visit Dharamsala, lying under the shadow of the Dhauladhar. The highest point in the Kangra Valley, Dharamsala is dominated by the towering mass of the Dhauladhar, its snowy peak rising from forests of oak, pine, cedar and deodar. After the British annexation of the Punjab in 1849, a cantonment town, Dharamsala, sprang up along the slopes of the Dhauladhar and in 1852 it became their administrative capital for the region. Lower Dharamsala is the district headquarters, while McLeodganj and Forsythganj occupy the higher reaches. Dharamsala still retains vestiges of its colonial past. At Forsythganj, is the Church of St John in the Wilderness where lies the grave of the British Viceroy, Lord Elgin, who died in 1863. Surrounded by towering deodars, this gray stone church is a handsome example of colonial architecture. Dharamsala was also home to one of the prime players of the Great Game, Francis Younghusband whose parents lived in Forsythganj in 1856.

After the devastation caused by the 1905 earthquake, Dharamsala's importance diminished, until Pandit Jawaharlal Nehru, India's first prime minister, gave asylum to His Holiness,

The Dalai Lama. In 1960, McLeodganj became the seat of the Tibetan Government-in-Exile and in the last five decades it has become Little Lhasa. Several thousand Tibetans settled in and around this area and built schools, monasteries, temples so that along the streets of 'Dhasa' (Dharamsala and Lhasa), there is an endless parade of maroon-robed monks, Tibetans in chubas, adorned with large chunks of turquoise and twirling prayer wheels. Colourful prayer flags flutter through the deodars and the sunlight illuminates the gilded roofs of the temples.

The next station is Chamunda and the temple is about four kilometres away. The temple of Chamunda is about seven hundred years old. Set against the panoramic view of the Dhauladhar, this modern temple on the banks of the Baner river, attracts thousands of devotees .Chamunda Devi is yet another powerful Shaktipitha and also one of the seven Matrikas (mother goddesses).

From Paror station, the train crisscrosses the road to Palampur, traversing through scenic pine forests. A few stations later, one reaches Maranda, the halt for Palampur. At Maranda, the Railway Guest House, perched on a hill, is a heritage building. Interestingly, the architects of the KVR ensured that a similar architectural style prevailed for all the stations en route. The style is a hybrid of the local kathkundi, horizontal deodar sleepers packed with stone—ideal for seismic areas—with British Elizabethan decorative elements. The stations, therefore, look like cottages with thin walls, wooden trusses, sloping roofs and deep verandahs held up by wooden pillars.

Palampur, the tehsil headquarters, is surrounded by tea gardens and lush green vistas against the snowcapped backdrop of the Dhauladhar. Today Palampur is a bustling town, and except for its administrative centre, much of the colonial buildings have been replaced by tall concrete structures. Yet, the surroundings are still green with tea bushes, interspersed with pine. Nearby is the Himachal Pradesh Agricultural University, offering courses in agriculture, veterinary and animal sciences, home science and basic sciences.

From Palampur the train travels through villages and fields, past the stations of Patti Rajpura, Panchrukhi and Majheran Himachal until it reaches Baijnath-Paprola. The steepest section of the line is from here to Ahju and, since 1976, the powerful ZDM3 locomotive built by Chittaranjan Locomotives has been used. These locomotives are especially designed for hilly regions and the train bogeys are reduced to only four carriages. The train begins to climb and high up, overlooking the Binwa river is the temple of Baijnath, dedicated to Siva, as Lord of the Physicians.

From Baijnath–Paprola the train goes across the Bhir gorge to Ahju (1210m), the highest point in the journey. Ahju, dominated by a medieval fort belonging to the Banghalia Pals, has one the most charming stations on the KVR. It is in the local kathkundi style with deep eaves and extremely well maintained The station is perched high above the railway line and so one has to descend several steps to the platform, comfortably equipped with benches affording grand sweeping view of the fort. Who would not like to pass the day at such a station?

From Ahju, one can visit Bir and Billing. Bir is set among tea gardens, lush and beautiful and the road, lined with rhododendron forests, takes one up to Billing, the take-off point for the popular sport of paragliding. Bir has a large Tibetan colony, several monasteries and a growing cottage industry for carpet weaving. Bir is also home to the Deer Park Institute, the vision of Dzongskar Khyentse Rinpoche. Established in 2006, this unique institute is where the study of Buddhism as well as other traditions of Indian philosophy are disseminated.

The last lap of the journey from the tiny station of Ahju takes one to Chauntra, a village which has grown into small town proportions. Largely agrarian, Chauntra and the neighbouring villages have fine examples of traditional architecture. This part of the journey is perhaps the most beautiful as the train glides through verdant landscapes with terraced rice field, orchards and slate-roofed, half-timber, double-storeyed villages, and increasing numbers of greenhouses, as the local Kangra farmer is now cultivating exotic Chinese cabbage, broccoli and herbs to cater to the international residents who rent houses in the villages. The final sweep is across a shallow ravine and Joginder Nagar comes into view.

Joginder Nagar came into prominence in the 1930s when the first hydroelectric power station was built. The Shanan Power House and the railway line grew together as men and materials were brought by rail to build the reservoir at Barot on the top of a hill. Today there are three power stations—Shanon, Bassi and Uhl. These power stations use the water of a single river, Uhl. A trolley takes one up the mountain, which offers a magnificent view of the district.

Joginder Nagar was once the biggest potato market in the area, where mules brought sack-loads of potatoes from Mandi, Kulu, Lahaul and Spiti for transportation to Bengal. It continues to be a market town and people from the neighbouring villages still come to buy their provisions, cloth and seeds.

Our journey ends in Joginder Nagar, a largish station with the crossbeam design more pronounced recalling cottages in England. The station has a small rest room with an attached bathroom for railway officials to spend a night or two. One still remembers the clean comfort of such rest rooms where one passed a night listening to the trains arrive and depart—memories of a cherished past.

The KVR comes to a halt here and in about thirty minutes, it turns around to begin its descent to the plains. The excitement of arrival and departure of the train at this end of the line station comes to a halt as the train sweeps out of the platform and into the tangle of field and forest.

Railnama
Chirodeep Chaudhuri

Delhi Junction
Devinder Singh

Railway's Filmy Chakkar
Photographs courtesy: Western Railway

Blast from the Past: Advertising on Trains and Platforms

Part 3
PHOTOGRAPHIC FEATURES

Railnama

CHIRODEEP CHAUDHURI

For me, the photographs I have been shooting, off and on, for the past 15 years are no different from the notes my friends who are writers make in their notepads. Mostly, the picture starts out as some detail I'd like to store away in my head. A few are like a hurriedly made scribble. Sometimes these act as the trigger leading me to expand on thoughts or ideas, which have continued to preoccupy me. A lot many others remain like scratched out comments that have, after time, made new sense.

Boredom is an unavoidable part of every commuter's experience but I have now devised ways of keeping myself both occupied and entertained. Photography, I've found, is one such way. For any alert photographer and one who is interested in the tragicomic drama of human life, the trains can be an inexhaustible mine of stories.

These pictures you will see are out-takes from many hours spent in the trains.

Outside the Chhatrapati Shivaji Terminus (CST), formerly Victoria Terminus (VT), Mumbai ➢

A mural by Satyajit Ray outside Central Metro Station, Kolkata.

CST Mumbai

On the Tapovan Express.

Railway timetable at Khopoli, Maharashtra.

Mumbai's local trains are the lifeline of the city.

Shatabdi Express (Amritsar to Delhi).

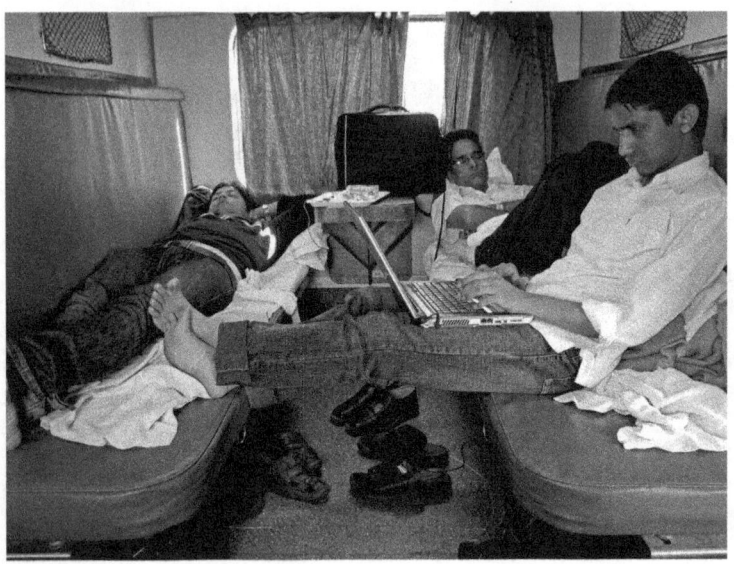

August Kranti Express (Mumbai to Delhi).

Delhi Junction

DEVINDER SINGH

Two world records were set on 8 February 1999. First, the largest route relay interlocking system in the world at that time became operational at Old Delhi railway station (or Delhi Junction). This was also the day when the remodelling of Delhi Junction had been completed. For the first time in its history, the station had remained completely empty—no passengers, trains, engines, hawkers or porters—for 44 hours.

Second—and totally unrelated to the above—was the record set in Ferozeshah Kotla cricket stadium by bowling legend Anil Kumble when he took 10 wickets in an innings in a test match against Pakistan, which India won.

These photographs, shot by Devinder Singh, an Indian Railway Traffic Service officer (who was then serving as Senior Divisional Operations Manager/Planning, Delhi Division, Northern Railway), capture the station on that day.

Railways' Filmy Chakkar

Photographs courtesy: Western Railway

'The trains keep going, the films keep rolling, and we watch in fascination as our lives play out on the parallel tracks that meet somewhere in the distance, somewhere out at infinity.'

—Jerry Pinto

Imran Khan and Sonakshi Sinha in Once Upon A Time In Mumbai–Again.

Ranvir Kapoor and Kalki Koechlin in Yeh Jawani Hai Deewani.

Sunny Deol in a local train.

Amitabh Bachchan in a local train for the promotion of Kaun Banega Crorepati.

Emran Hashmi in Ghanchakkar.

Shahid Kapoor and Padmini Kolhapure in Phata Poster Nikla Hero.

Blast from the Past: Advertising on Trains and Platforms

'Railway stations emerged as nerve centres for commercial activity. Shops and markets came up around them and even the best and biggest advertising hoardings were often put up on the front façades of railway stations to ensure maximum visibility.'

—Sandipan Deb

Different railways promoting travel on their lines.

...dings of Murphy Radio and others on top of the Madras Central railway station.

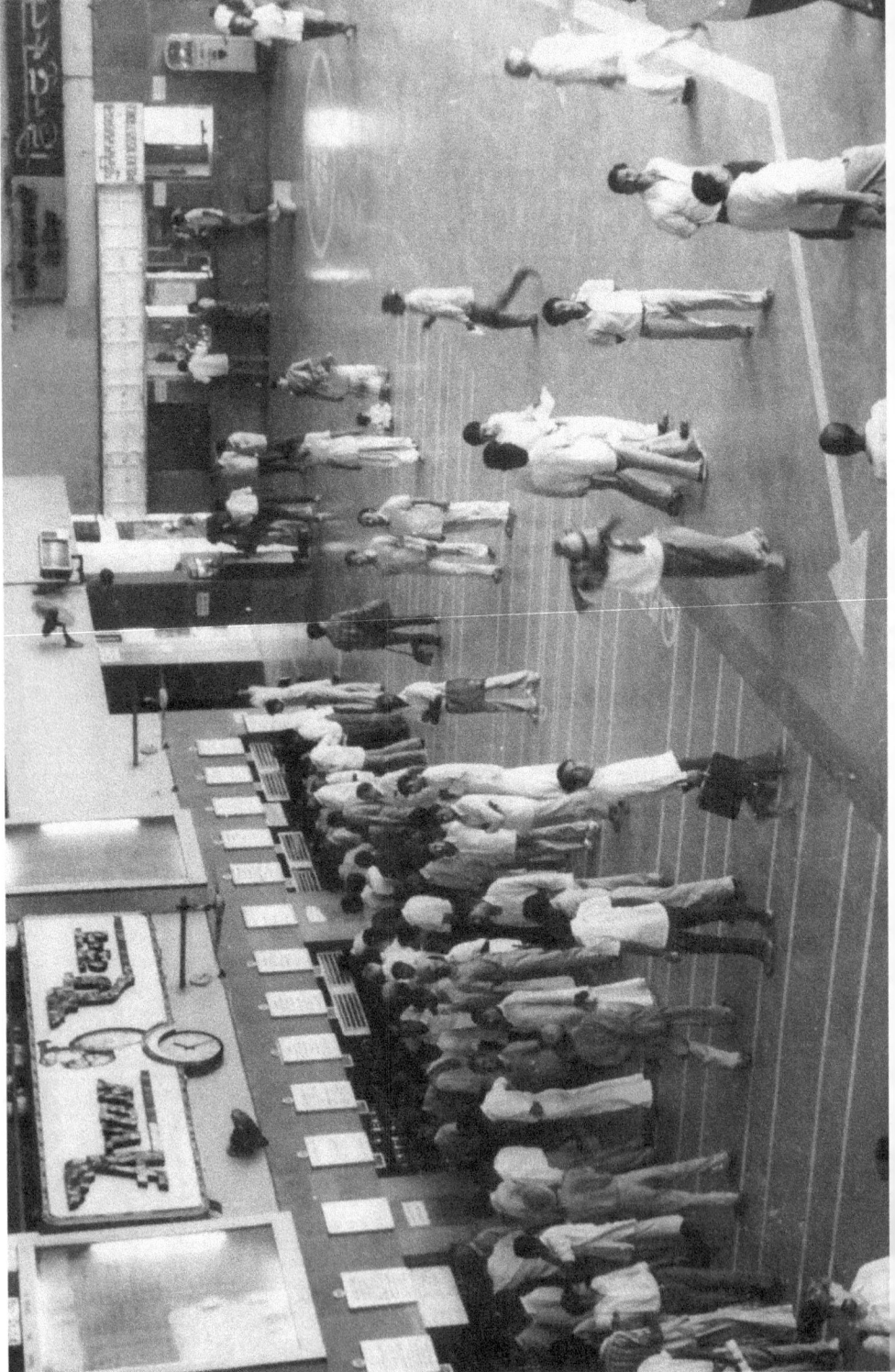

CONTRIBUTORS

AASHEESH SHARMA, a senior journalist based in Delhi, is currently Associate Editor of *Hindustan Times Brunch*. Prior to this, he worked with NDTV, *India Today*, *The Times of India*, *Financial Express* and *The Pioneer*, at various points over the past two decades.

BISWADEEP GHOSH has worked with leading publications such as *Outlook*, *Hindustan Times*, Magna Publishing and *The Times of India*. Among his books are biographies of Shah Rukh Khan, Salman Khan, Aishwarya Rai and Hrithik Roshan, published by Magna Publishing as part of its Hall of Fame series. His books of children's fiction—*Woof! Woof!* and its sequel *My Brother Jack*—were published by the Times Group Books. Consulting Editor with Samay Live and an op-ed page writer for *Mail Today*, Biswadeep has contributed to several other books, magazines and newspapers. He is presently working on the biography of the Indian cricket captain, M.S. Dhoni.

CHIRODEEP CHAUDHURI started his career in journalism as a trainee reporter. It was his way of trying to get a foot in the door. His next job—his first as a photographer—was with the Sunday Observer Group in Mumbai. Since then he has worked on the teams of one of India's premier magazine groups (The Outlook Group), travelled the length and breath of India as a photographer and picture editor for a travel website (traveljini.com). Currently, he is working as the picture editor for the international arts and culture magazine (*Timeout*) for their India editions.

His works have been published in books and magazines around the world. He has also travelled extensively in India and also in the USA, UK and China and is part of the permanent collections of the Peabody Essex Museum, Salem (USA), Museum of Photographic Arts, Houston (USA), and the Kiyosato Museum of Photographic Arts (Japan) and many private collections in India.

GILLIAN WRIGHT is a journalist, author and translator who has spent most of her life in New Delhi with her partner Mark Tully. She has collaborated with him on all his books. A student of Indian languages, her translations include the modern Hindi classics *Raag Darbari* by Shrilal Shukla and Rahi Masoom Reza's epic novel of pre and post-partition rural eastern Uttar Pradesh, *Adha Gaon*, published in English as *A Village Divided*.

Her other books include *The Darjeeling Tea Book*, on the history and the mysteries of Darjeeling tea, and an *Introduction to the Hill Stations of India*.

IAN J. KERR is a senior academic at the University of Manitoba and a Professorial Research Associate, History, SOAS. Ian is also a leading authority on Indian Railways on which he has written extensively including *Building the Railways of the Raj 1850-1900* and *Engines of Change: the Railroads that made India*.

JERRY PINTO lives and works in Mumbai. He has been a mathematics tutor, school librarian, journalist and columnist. His first novel, *Em and the Big Hoom*, launched to great reviews, and last year he received the Hindu Lit for Life award. Pinto has also authored other books, including *Helen: The Life and Times of an H-Bomb*, which won the National Award for the Best Book on Cinema in 2006; a book for children titled *A Bear for Felicia* and a graphic novel called *When Crows are White*.

Pinto is on the board of MelJol, an NGO that works in the sphere of child rights and teaches journalism at the Sophia Institute for Social Communications Media. He tweets under the handle mahimkajerry

KARTIK IYENGAR is the author of the bestselling *Horn OK Please* series. Besides being a successful corporate professional, he is also an adrenaline junkie who has tried everything from scuba diving and bungee jumping to daring the climatic extremes of the globe. A compulsive travel hog, a heavy metal maniac and an ardent social media digerati, Kartik has thousands of hyperactive hopper fans on http://www.facebook.com/hopfans

CONTRIBUTORS

He actively promotes and contributes a part of his book earnings to two organizations: Tibetan SOS Children's Village in Ladakh and the Mahesh Memorial Cancer Foundation.

SIR MARK TULLY was born in Calcutta, India, in 1935. He was the Chief of Bureau, BBC, New Delhi, for twenty-two years, was knighted in the New Year's Honours list in 2002 and was awarded the Padma Bhushan in 2005. Today, his distinguished broadcasting career includes being the regular presenter of the contemplative BBC Radio 4 programme *Something Understood*. His books include *No Full stops in India*, *The Heart of India*, *India in Slow Motion* (written with his partner and colleague Gillian Wright), and *India's Unending Journey*. He lives in New Delhi.

OMAIR AHMAD is the author of *Jimmy, the Terrorist* (winner of the Vodafone Crossword Award for Fiction and shortlisted for the Man Asian Literary Prize) and *The Storyteller's Tale*. He grew up in Saudi Arabia and India, and has been a journalist, policy analyst and semi-employed in a variety of odd vocations in a few countries. He currently lives in New Delhi.

PREMOLA GHOSE is Chief, Programme Division at the India International Centre, New Delhi. She writes regularly for different magazines, including *India Magazine*, *Swagat*, *Seminar*, among others. Premola has also written and illustrated three children's books: *Tales of Historic Delhi* (2011, Zubaan and Amber Press); *The Magical Ride of Juley the Camel* (2011, Amber Books); *Zero goes to Goa* (2014, Amber Books).

RUSKIN BOND has been writing for over sixty years, and has now over 120 titles in print—novels, collections of stories, poetry, essays, anthologies and books for children. His first novel, *The Room on the Roof*, received the prestigious John Llewellyn Rhys award in 1957. He has also received the Padma Shri, and two awards from the Sahitya Akademi—one for his short stories and another for his writings for children. In 2012, the Delhi government gave him its Lifetime Achievement Award.

Born in 1934, Ruskin Bond grew up in Jamnagar, Shimla, New Delhi and Dehradun. Apart from three years in the UK, he has spent all his life in India, and now lives in Mussoorie with his adopted family.

A shy person, Ruskin says he likes being a writer because, 'When I'm writing there's nobody watching me. Today, it's hard to find a profession where you're not being watched!'

SANDIPAN DEB is an IIT-IIM graduate who wandered into journalism after reading a quote from filmmaker George Lucas—"Everyone's cage door is open"—and has stayed there (in journalism, not a cage) since 1990. He has been Managing Editor of *Outlook*, Editor of *The Financial Express*, and the Founder-Editor of *Open* magazine.

Currently, he is an independent writer/editor, and Managing Partner of Aardvark Media, a boutique media-agnostic publishing house.

Sandipan is the author of three books. *The IITians: The story of an extraordinary Indian institution and how its alumni are transforming the world*, was published in 2004. *Fallen Angel: The making and unmaking of Rajat Gupta*, and his novel, *The Last War*, a re-imagining of the Mahabharata set in the Mumbai underworld, were both published in December 2012.

sandipanonline.com collects much of his writings in the media in one place and is where he blogs.

SHARMILA KANTHA is the author of *Building India with Partnership: The Story of CII 1895-2005*. Her other publications include two novels, *Just the Facts, Madamji* and *A Break in the Circle*.

SHOBA NARAYAN is an award-winning author and columnist. In the past, she has written for *The New York Times, Wall Street Journal, Washington Post, Newsweek*, Knowledge@Wharton, and other publications. She was awarded the Pulitzer Fellowship at the Columbia Journalism School. She is the author of two memoirs: *Monsoon Diary: A Memoir with Recipes* and *Return to India*.

www.ingramcontent.com/pod-product-compliance
Lightning Source LLC
Chambersburg PA
CBHW020745160426
43192CB00006B/254